Praise for *Switchers*

"Wondering how to get your career from here to *there*? Dr. Dawn Graham gives you the best process I've ever seen. She's an expert on how to make your value visible in your new niche. And you'll love her plain language. Take a look at her sample scripts in Chapter 9—she shows you what to say in all kinds of tricky networking situations. Dawn is the best career switch expert you could ever read or hope for."

—Lynne Waymon, CEO of Contacts Count LLC, and coauthor of *Strategic Connections* and *Make Your Contacts Count*

"*Switchers* is a masterwork. Utilizing her strong clinical skills, Dr. Graham gets underneath the anxiety associated with changing careers and divides the process into digestible, achievable steps. Then, too, she helps the reader use psychology toward convincing others that this switch is an investment worth making. This is an indispensable guide to mastering the territory that's essential for people to reinvent themselves."

—Dr. Jody Foster, MD, MBA, Clinical Associate Professor of Psychiatry in the Perelman School of Medicine at the University of Pennsylvania; Chair of the Department of Psychiatry at Pennsylvania Hospital; and author of *The Schmuck in My Office: How to Deal Effectively with Difficult People at Work*

"Dawn Graham's expertise as a psychologist, recruiter, and career coach has all coalesced into a fantastic guide for career switchers. Anyone even considering being a career switcher ought to read and follow Dawn's advice. I'll be recommending this highly accessible book to all the students I coach at Kellogg."

—Adnan Rukieh, Director, Career Services, Kellogg School of Management at Northwestern University

"Changing jobs today is hard enough. But if your goal is a complete career change, you won't stand a chance using the same old job techniques. Dawn Graham's tested, step-by-savvy-step proce making a life-changing career switch is as real as it gets. There instant, phony, click-your-way tricks here. Graham will put work—using detailed methods rooted in her expertise in execu cruiting, coaching, and psychology—and, ultimately, *Switchers* you to work in the new career you want. Career change is a hu but Graham shows you exactly how to make it real."

—Nick Corcodilos, asktheheadhun

"I have people come to me all the time for guidance in changing careers. Sometimes they know what they want to do and sometimes they just want something different, but they don't know what. Regardless, they don't know how to switch gears. Dawn Graham helpfully goes through the whole process—including figuring out just what you're willing to give up for the change (Are you willing to take a pay cut? Move?); how to get around the ever-present applicant tracking systems; and how to take responsibility for your own career. If you're looking to change careers, but just not sure how to go about it, this book will be immensely helpful. Switching careers isn't easy, but it *is* possible."

—Suzanne Lucas, The Evil HR Lady

"*Switchers* is not just a book—it's an easy-to-read map for your career journey that will guide you down the path towards a successful switch."

—Amber Wigmore Alvarez, Executive Director,
Talent and Careers, IE Business School

"So few people are in jobs they truly love, depriving them of a truly fulfilling career experience, and the world of their gifts and talents. In a fun and engaging style, Graham offers readers the tools to stand out from the pack and bridge that gap."

—Randy Street, President at GH Smart and coauthor
of *New York Times* bestseller *Who: The A Method for Hiring*

"The insight in *Switchers* is exceptional. It's like reading Dr. Dawn's radio show and feeling like she's talking directly to you! With this book you'll get candid and very expert advice on making a career change. Having helped thousands of people find new careers, I promise you, this book is a must-read."

—Tom Gimbel, Founder and CEO of LaSalle Network

SWITCHERS

HOW SMART PROFESSIONALS
CHANGE CAREERS—AND SEIZE SUCCESS

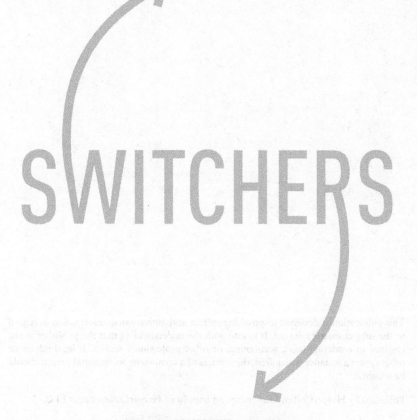

SWITCHERS

• DAWN GRAHAM •

HARPERCOLLINS
LEADERSHIP

An Imprint of HarperCollins

This publication is designed to provide accurate and authoritative information in regard to the subject matter covered. It is sold with the understanding that the publisher is not engaged in rendering legal, accounting, or other professional service. If legal advice or other expert assistance is required, the services of a competent professional person should be sought.

Published by HarperCollins Leadership, an imprint of HarperCollins Focus LLC.

Library of Congress Control Number: 2018003832.

ISBN: 9780814439630
E-ISBN: 9780814439654

This book is dedicated to my father—
my motivation in everything.

CONTENTS

ACKNOWLEDGMENTS

With each passing year, it becomes clearer to me how past experiences influence the present. The subconscious mind holds a treasure trove of memories that shape our daily actions and create infinite ripple effects. To that end, I want to thank everyone who is a part of the current that led to the writing of this book.

With special thanks to: My father, who challenged me every step of the way while being there to catch me without fail when I stumbled. You may have left this world still believing I need someone to take care of me, but it's because of you that I don't. My mother (and volunteer proofreader!), who continues to be my closest friend and confidante. You taught me planning, patience, and excellence, and practice them to a level I will never attain. Ginger, ChaCha, and Aunt, strong women who blazed a trail for me early in life and sustained me as I traveled my own path. My extended family, who, despite us all being caught up in our own busy lives, will always be with me on my journey. My dear friends in New Jersey, Minnesota, Colorado, Washington, D.C., Illinois, and Pennsylvania—places I've lived, worked, grown, and probably got a speeding ticket. You've taught me that home is about the *who*, not the where. Kevin and Donna, who've seen it all and still stand by me. Art Berman, my constant cheerleader, benevolent critic, vigilant brand guardian, and dear friend. There is no role you haven't played on this journey, and words fall short in saying thank you. Susie Brock, your leadership wisdom lives on through this book. Cynthia McRae, my doctoral advisor, dissertation chair, and first professor of career theory. And Lily, who mostly just got in the way, but whom I adore anyhow.

My first-stage editors, Suzanne Murray and Rachel Fending at Style Matters, who helped transform a choppy PowerPoint into something that looked like an actual book. My agent, Lorin Rees, who got 'er done. Seth Schulman, my proposal editor, and Shawn Rodgers, who made my amateur graphics book-ready over and over.

The team at AMACOM, who coached me through the process patiently as a first-timer, especially Ellen Kadin, a true professional who explained every step along the way, sometimes twice if I needed it. Lynne Waymon, for writing the original networking book, *Make Your Contacts Count*, which changed me from an introvert to an introvert who networks, and Steve Dalton, for writing the book that erases ambiguity from the most unstructured part of the job search (*The 2-Hour Job Search*). These books have paved the way for all job seekers.

Nick Corcodilos (aka "Ask the Headhunter"), for your encouragement and generous coaching, and Ross MacPherson, resume guru and Mosquitos fan. My esteemed colleagues in the MBACSWP for being a sounding board and inspiring new ideas. I am privileged to be on the Board of such a talented and dedicated group of giving individuals. Julie Cohen and Ford Myers, who are both incredible career and leadership coaches, and were kind enough to mentor me when I was an intern getting started in this field. Scott Sill, the most well-connected guy I know: thank you for the many introductions, especially those that led to publishing this book. Kay Rock, who gave me my first shot at outplacement decades ago, which inspired my career in careers. The Dream Team, Michelle Stucker and Dion Simpkins at Career Talk; the staff at SiriusXM111; and all the expert guests who share their wisdom on the radio every week. The show's listeners, blog subscribers, Twitter followers, and the countless career clients who honed my skills and brand. You've made me a better career coach and provided the motivation to write this book, creating a ripple effect that will help many others succeed on the paths that you, too, have taken.

My team and family at WEMBA, who have made me laugh every day that I've been working at Wharton. With special thanks to Steve Hernandez and Carina Myers, my partners in crime, for keeping me (mostly) sane; Mary Gross, for paving the way and continuing to be a steadfast partner; and the executive students who push me to raise the bar year after year.

To Epic Church for working against the odds each week to reach every person in the city. To the countless individuals who have offered advice, criticism, and ideas: I've taken every piece of feedback to heart, even if I didn't ultimately follow it. And finally, to those who said "yes" when I asked to network (especially if I asked to "pick your brain"—for which I apologize profusely). I'm a firm believer that we take something away from every interaction, and your feedback and insights are woven into everything I've become.

Preface

If you're like most Americans, you will spend around *five years* of your life engaged in some type of job search activity. You'll hold about eleven different positions in the course of your career, and each job search might take you six months or longer.[1] The new normal is not only to switch *jobs* but to change *professions*—which isn't easy to accomplish. When you want to make a 180-degree change, you need a savvy understanding of the art and science of the job search. That's where *Switchers* comes in.

Switchers goes beyond the basic tips you've likely heard (and tried) before. Calling on my background as a psychologist, former recruiter, and career coach, I'll give you tools to land the job you really want, even if you aren't a "traditional" candidate with the expected or standard career trajectory for the role. *Switchers* will demystify the job search process and provide simple strategies for getting in front of the decision makers and securing the job you want.

Just to clarify, "simple" is not the same as "easy." In our one-click world of instant access, job seekers might expect the same ease in the job search process. Technology has become a seductress, luring candidates into endless hours of internet searches and countless online applications. These methods are barely effective for even the most qualified job applicants, and career *changers* who rely on them don't stand a chance.

Career Switchers tend to give up *not* because they lack the skills to excel in their desired profession, but because they don't have the proper search strategies and knowledge. I've written *Switchers* to change that pattern. This is the first book to specifically address the unique needs and job search challenges of career *changers*, who are ready to make their new career a reality, but are unsure of how to do it. If you've picked this book up, chances are you've done your soul searching and know *where* you want to go—you just need a road map for getting there.

As the Career Director for The Wharton School's MBA Program for Executives, I've built a brand as the career coach for some of the world's leading business minds, many of whom not only are career changers, but also are vying for some of the most competitive jobs. I also host the weekly show *Career Talk* on Sirius XM radio, advising people across North America on the topics in this book.

The thirteen chapters in *Switchers* walk you through the sequential steps of the job search process. As you read, you'll find practical strategies, tips, and examples you can implement immediately. Each chapter also has several Switch Action items for further thought, so you may find it helpful to have a journal handy to reflect on these. You can read the book from cover-to-cover or skim through to focus on the specific topics that most apply to you.

I've filled this book with insider secrets from a recruiter's point of view, and have taken it one step further. With a dual background in recruiting and psychology, I've written *Switchers* to help you understand the psychological principles that underlie your own journey and also how hiring managers and recruiters think. Knowing what is happening on the other side of the desk gives you confidence and an advantage. You'll learn not just the questions they're asking themselves about you, but the subconscious connections and assumptions that *they* don't even realize they're making. You'll be able to leverage that information to your advantage by giving them what they don't even know they're looking for.

When you're trying to switch careers, you'll go through times of doubt when you question your decision, your competence, and your ability to succeed in a new identity. To help you move past these moments of uncertainty, *Switchers* addresses motivational challenges that often derail Switchers and offers ways to overcome them.

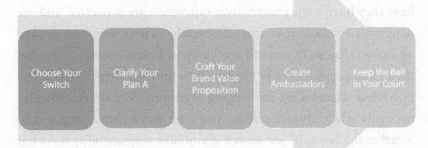

Your Career Switch Road Map

The Empowered Approach

To get optimal results in your career switch, it's important to approach the job search with an informed and empowered mindset. There are a few key elements to this way of thinking, and as you progress through *Switchers*, you'll notice four general mental themes that continue to emerge.

Responsibility

Reality

Risk

Resilience

Each of these is critical to your success—there are no shortcuts. By embracing these four foundational attitudes (The Four R's), you won't be tempted to throw in the towel when your dream is still within reach.

Responsibility

You will best engage your job search by adopting an internal "locus of control." This is a psychology term that describes how people view their circumstances. People who are oriented toward an *internal* locus of control take responsibility for their actions, believe they have some control over outcomes, are proactive, and are determined to find ways around obstacles. Those who lean toward an *external* locus of control are likely to blame outside forces for their circumstances, credit random luck for their successes, and feel powerless when facing challenging situations. As a result, they give up easily when obstacles arise. You'll be much better prepared to weather the "switch" job search if you take responsibility for what happens and have an internal locus of control. Without accepting responsibility, you will not *act* as needed to take charge of your switch.

Reality

People who attain success work with what *does* happen, not with what *should* happen. Sure, a company *should* contact you after an interview to say they are moving forward with another candidate, but sometimes they leave you hanging. Or a company may decide they want you to submit a video interview, which feels impersonal and awkward to you. Companies may lowball you during salary negotiations. Situations like these suck, but they happen. During your job search, things may seem unfair, silly, or inconvenient, but if you want the job you need to play the game and find creative ways around these realities. You will get further when you stop fighting and put your energy toward dealing with reality. If you can't accept reality, your actions will be *misdirected*.

Risk

There are no absolutes or guarantees in a switch. A job search is often ambiguous and anxiety-provoking, and you will be tempted to stay within your comfort zone. This is your brain's misguided effort to keep you safe from potential threats. You must overcome this to switch careers. Risks are inevitable when venturing into unchartered territory and the best rewards usually come from the greatest risks. Without guarantees, your brain might try to convince you that the switch is not worth it. Hold steady, especially when things get tough. Also guard against outlying situations that could mislead you to believe a process or strategy doesn't work. See them for what they are: one-off occurrences. Look for themes and patterns to recognize when you are rationalizing or making excuses for not doing something. Your brain may be trying to protect you from getting hurt. However, transformational change like a career switch is rarely possible without bumps and bruises. No risks, no *results*.

Resilience

At a basic level, the job switch is a series of human interactions that culminate in either an offer or a rejection. This process is rarely logical or linear, and is fraught with bias, assumptions, complexity, and rejection. Because of this, it's not enough to apply tactical strategies. Yes, sharpening your resume is important. But what will differentiate you and land you the job is understanding the psychology behind the search and being agile enough to engage your strengths to overcome obstacles. As long as your job search involves humans, it involves psychology, so resilience is a must. Without it, you'll run out of motivation to *persevere* when the road gets rocky.

The Four R's & Career Switch Success				
~~Responsibility~~	Responsibility	Responsibility	Responsibility	Responsibility
Reality	~~Reality~~	Reality	Reality	Reality
Risk	Risk	~~Risk~~	Risk	Risk
Resilience	Resilience	Resilience	~~Resilience~~	Resilience
NO ACTION	NO DIRECTION	NO RESULTS	NO PERSEVERANCE	CAREER SWITCH SUCCESS!

The Four R's

Ongoing Career Management

While a job search consists of a defined set of activities, *career management* is a fluid and ongoing process that includes regular networking and brand building, gaining new skills and experiences, and continuously evaluating the market to ensure the value you offer remains current. Many people don't make time for career management until facing a job search. But not only can it increase success in your current field, it can also make future job searches infinitely shorter and easier—especially if you skip the entire process and are directly recruited by someone in your network. So it's worth making time for routinely. *Switchers* includes simple steps for managing your career, both before and after you land your target job.

Switching careers can be a bumpy road, but it's worth it to be working in a role that aligns with your drive, values, and interests. You could keep waiting and planning, but you'll wind up wishing you had started today. So stop wishing and keep reading!

1

Choose Your Switch

Are You a Switcher?

The "Magic" Equation
for Seizing Career Success

Donna secretly dreamed of a career in the fast-paced world of advertising and media. Yet, here she was, forty years old and still grinding away at the same large bank in New York City as she had since she was twenty. With her family's support and encouragement, Donna decided to make a change. It was now or never. Without telling anyone at work, she began looking for a new job. Not just any new job—an entirely new career in advertising at a large media company. She knew she would probably have to sacrifice some of her salary, but she felt confident her impressive resume and stellar presentation skills would land her a well-paying role in her target area. After all, she was in New York, the world's media mecca. There was no better place to seek this exciting career opportunity.

Donna dusted off the resume she had last updated six years earlier when making an internal move by adding a few lines about her current job. She felt giddy when she searched the major online job sites and found senior roles open at CBS Corporation, HBO,

CNN, and major advertising agencies. She picked out seven roles that seemed ideal and submitted her resume. And then she waited. And waited.

After six weeks she still hadn't heard from a single company. What was going on? Confused, Donna picked up the phone to follow up with a few companies just to be certain they received her application. The recruiters she talked to were pleasant, but they delivered jarring news. While Donna had an impressive background, she "wasn't what they were looking for" because she didn't have "the right experience or industry contacts." Donna's background in finance was impressive but, as one recruiter bluntly put it, they were looking for a creative type—not a math whiz. Donna was dumbfounded that her resume wasn't even being considered and frustrated by wasting six weeks waiting for responses.

Donna had an old college acquaintance who worked at one of the companies, so she reached out to reconnect and see if he had any advice. Her contact was candid and told Donna the company only hired individuals who had come up through the ranks. If she wanted a senior role in advertising, she would need to start from the bottom and gain experience like everyone else. Donna felt discouraged, but rationalized that this was just a requirement of her friend's firm. Once she got an interview somewhere, she could share her many accomplishments and convince the hiring manager that she could learn the job.

Two months passed and still Donna hadn't gotten any traction. Not a single interview—just impersonal rejections, or worse, no responses at all. She considered returning to graduate school to get a master's degree in media studies, figuring this would boost her credibility. But with two preteen daughters, she didn't see how she could add schoolwork to her schedule. Then a neighbor connected her to a hiring manager at a small advertising firm and she got an interview. But she felt like she and the recruiter were speaking a different language, and she was never called back. Donna felt frustrated and resentful. She was on the verge of giving up and simply continuing with her standard routine, going through the motions at the bank. Why couldn't these companies see what a great candidate she was?

The Plight of the Switcher

If you're trying to make a major change, Donna's predicament probably sounds familiar. It's hard enough getting a new job in the *same* career, but most traditional job seekers know the basic steps and typically land new positions within six months. Switching careers is different. Like Donna, you face broader obstacles to landing the job of your dreams, such as an inability or unwillingness for recruiters to understand how transferable skills can provide great value. Career Switchers often don't strategize sufficiently up front. They don't land interviews because they underestimate the need to reframe their experience, network properly, and use social media to their advantage. When Switchers do land interviews, they often misjudge the preparation needed, so they come across as incongruent or unqualified. As rejections pile up, they become disheartened. Eventually, all too many give up.

That's unfortunate because unconventional career moves are easier to make than ever before. Globalization, technology advancement, the "gig economy," and a rise in portfolio careers and side hustles are usurping traditional career certainties. With corporate ladders, up-or-out mentalities, corner office cultures, and glass ceilings all under siege, more professionals can leap boldly into new careers—*if* they know how to defeat stereotypes, poor hiring practices, and outdated thinking. To get a hiring manager to roll the dice on you as a nontraditional hire, you must be prepared. Don't suffer Donna's fate. In this chapter, you'll:

- Take an honest look at the sacrifices you're willing to make for the new career you want

- Determine whether a career switch is right for you at this point
- Learn the classic pitfalls career Switchers need to watch out for
- Discover the "magic" equation for seizing career success

What Type of Switcher Are You?

Many people who want to switch careers underestimate the nature of the challenge they're accepting. Before doing anything else, take time to think about what type of career Switcher you are. There is more than one type, and some switches are considerably more difficult than others. Here's the basic principle to keep in mind: *The further you stray from a "traditional" career trajectory, the harder it is to switch.* Knowing the degree of difficulty will help you design your strategy.

An *industry switch* is moderately challenging. I made this type of switch myself when I transitioned from corporate to academia. As a corporate recruiter, I understood the skills and lingo of helping people shift in their careers, but I lacked direct experience applying those skills to an academic setting, where the structure, culture, resources, and outcomes differed significantly. So, when interviewing, it was incumbent upon me to prove to the hiring team that my functional knowledge was applicable, and demonstrate how I would adapt and navigate effectively in an unfamiliar industry. Interviewers asked me about this directly, and I got an offer largely because I anticipated this and prepared a concrete, outcome-based response.

Making a *functional switch* within the same industry is more challenging than an industry shift. Jessica was an accounting manager in the pharmaceutical industry who wanted to stay in pharma and become a marketing manager. Her familiarity with the industry helped a lot, but she needed new knowledge, skills, and credentials to market medications to prescribing physicians. It was a lot different than keeping the books straight. So with the support of her boss, Jessica sought out special projects inside of the company where she could gain hands-on skills by working with the marketing team. This ultimately put her on the right path to complete the switch.

	DEGREE OF DIFFICULTY	
	FUNCTIONAL SKILLS	
INDUSTRY EXPERIENCE	3. Very Challenging "Single Switcher - Function"	1. Least Challenging "Non Switcher - Traditional Candidate"
	4. Extremely Challenging "Double Switcher - Function & Industry"	2. Moderately Challenging "Single Switcher - Industry"

Types of Career Switch by Degrees of Difficulty

To make a functional switch, you will likely need to find someone to advocate for you. Before you begin a job search, you may need to gain direct experience through volunteering, pursuing applied training, or working in a self-created "internship" similar to Jessica. A functional switch can be easier if you do it within your current organization. If you have a track record of doing exceptional work with the company, they might be willing to put in extra effort to train you rather than conduct an expensive external candidate search or risk losing you as a loyal employee.

The hardest switch to make is the *double switch*—a professional who makes *both* an industry and functional change at once. This includes Donna, who wanted to switch from a finance role at the bank to an advertising role in media, or the newspaper editor whose job became obsolete so he followed his dream of working as a brand marketer in a startup, and the corporate attorney turned human resources executive in a growing nonprofit.

It comes as no surprise that double Switchers tend to become frustrated quickly. My friend Kevin, who joined the military after completing a degree in computer science, served eight years in the navy, where he earned the rank of lieutenant. Ready for a change, Kevin pursued civilian roles in large tech companies as a supply chain manager. Hiring managers were impressed by his noteworthy assignments in Afghanistan, but they had difficulty figuring out where Kevin's skills would fit in their departments. Disheartened but not deterred, Kevin changed his approach and began describing his military experience in language that corporations understood. He created a strategy to network with individuals within the companies he was targeting, many of whom had made similar transitions, and he practiced relaying his value in mock interviews. He did the work *for* hiring managers instead of relying on them to figure out how his background might contribute.

A double switch requires persistence, courage, and sacrifice, but it's completely doable. The key to success is to adopt a unique and tailored strategy, which I will help you develop in this book.

Think about your own goals. What type of a Switcher are you? Are you attempting a leap that's farther than you thought? Have you underestimated the difficulty? If you're not quite sure yet, don't worry. The exercises in the next few chapters will help you define your focus with greater clarity. Then you can figure out how high the mountain is that you must climb.

Clinging to How Things Are

An old fable about a hunter who sets a trap to capture a monkey offers a perfect analogy for your biggest obstacle as a Switcher. The hunter puts food in a glass jar with a narrow opening. When the hungry monkey comes along and reaches into the jar to grab the food, he is unable to remove his paw since his *closed* fist doesn't fit back out through the hole. Although the monkey could simply let go of the food and remove his paw from the jar to escape, he instead chooses to cling tightly, and is captured by the hunter.

Sometimes we are unable to let go of what is keeping us trapped, even when achieving freedom could be simple. Switchers are excited to make a major change, but many aren't so jazzed about the sacrifices that often come with it—like taking a salary cut, dropping levels on the organizational chart, or relocating to another city. We grow attached to our comfortable lives and don't want to give them up—or at least certain parts of them. So we cling to our current identity, without even recognizing it. And the more scared we get, the more we cling, and the less likely we are to reach our goals. Identity clinging is one of the most important obstacles I will cover in this book.

As Switchers, we need to get real with ourselves first. We must acknowledge that many parts of our current careers that we like—such as salary, title, or status—will change. (I'll discuss more about career identity in Chapter Two.) The good news is we don't have to relinquish everything, just some things. Ask yourself, "What are my *true* non-negotiables?" Non-negotiables are requirements you are 100 percent certain you cannot forego, no matter what. These are different from ideals or wants. All of us are shooting for the ideal job, and we all have a list of wants a mile long. But many of us haven't thought hard about what we *must* have in our new careers to be happy.

Maybe you're divorced and have dual custody of young children, so you can't relocate out of state. Or maybe you have a chronic health condition and you must limit your search to employers who offer sufficient medical insurance coverage. Maybe you're a single parent or a primary caregiver for an aging relative, so frequent travel isn't something you can do. Some situations truly are inflexible, and they may present additional hurdles to navigate. These are your non-negotiables.

Please don't let these stop you. Limitations can lead to the creative solutions, and persistence will take you far. No matter what, you're never *truly* stuck. I'll discuss this more soon.

Most of us have very few, if any, true non-negotiables. We might not *want* to forego the comfortable salary, four weeks of vacation we've earned, private office, reputation as the "go-to" guy, or flexible schedule. But we *would* be willing to sacrifice these perks for a successful switch. And, keep in mind that some challenges might prove temporary. David accepted a demotion at a top company to "learn the ropes" in a different function, only to be recruited two years later into a prestigious role at a smaller company. At this new job, he made more money than before his switch. So, don't lose perspective. A step back in the short run might catapult you ahead in the long run, especially if passion is fueling you.

If you're serious about a switch, you can alter spending habits, rebuild your vacation bank, or relocate to a new place. And if you aren't willing to make any sacrifices, it may be a sign switching isn't right for you.

SWITCH ACTION

The Career Switch Tolerance Questionnaire

SIT DOWN TO SOUL-SEARCH about your non-negotiables and wants, making use of this Career Switch Tolerance Questionnaire. As you answer the questions, be realistic and honest. Maybe your current job offers more value than you thought. If so, it's better to know that now. Everything in life entails a trade-off, and only you can decide what's most important. But if you tally your score and find you're willing to adjust your lifestyle, then great news: This book will hand you the keys to your future!

Think about the time, effort, and sacrifice you are willing to make *at this time* to support your career change. For each statement, indicate the *degree of your willingness to change* on a scale of 0 through 5, where 0 indicates "No way," and 5 indicates "Yes, absolutely." The questions in parentheses help you think about each item more deeply.

→ Are you willing to lose money or accept a pay decrease? (How much?)

→ Are you willing to relocate? (How far?)

→ Are you willing to take a lower position? (How much lower?)

→ Are you willing to put daily effort into your goal and be disciplined? (For how long?)

→ Are you willing to make pursuing your goal a significant priority over other goals? (How much time per week?)

→ Are you willing to spend time or money to earn additional licenses, certifications, or clearances? (How much?)

→ Are you willing to live on savings for a time? (How long?)

→ Are you willing to travel up to five days per week or 80 percent of the time? (For how long?)

→ Are you willing to proactively network (events, meetings, conferences, phone calls)? (How many per week?)

→ Are you willing to accept dead ends or rebuffs without becoming frustrated? (How will you do this?)

→ Are you willing to give up time with friends, family, and hobbies? (How much?)

→ Are you willing to give up control of your schedule (autonomy) and driving your tasks in your new job? (How much, for how long?)

Results

Mostly 0s or 1s: This may not be the best time to make a significant career move where there is great risk or change.

Mostly 2s or 3s: Certain sacrifices may be tolerable in a career move, while others are not. Be sure to align your career goals accordingly.

Mostly 4s or 5s: You are likely open to significant risk and willing to put in whatever is required to reach your career goal.

Regret Cuts Deepest

Depending on what you learned from the Career Switch Tolerance Questionnaire, you might feel ready to tackle the big switch. Or you might feel somewhat uncertain and inclined to do additional introspecting. If you're more apprehensive than you thought, take a few days to think in depth about what is non-negotiable. You might start to see creative options emerge where you least expected them.

Let's say you're a corporate technology manager who earns over $100,000 a year and you think you just can't afford a significant pay cut to work at a nonprofit. Over the next few days, review your household budget in detail. Where does your paycheck currently go? What flexibility can you build in, even if just temporarily? There might be a few extras—a $215 monthly cable bill, annual vacations abroad—that you'd willingly sacrifice for the job of your dreams. Maybe you could take a second job temporarily to make up for a portion of the pay cut, or spend a year saving $20,000 before you officially embark on a switch. Other options might include downsizing your home, giving up your car in favor of public transit, or renting out your basement on AirBnB.

If none of these appeal to you, either you're not as interested in this career switch as you may have thought, or you just need to get creative! When I decided to switch careers in my early thirties, I sold my loft and moved into an ancient (marketed as "charming with a lot of character") apartment with some freeloading roaches for roommates. Yuck! I became my local dollar store's best customer and clipping coupons became a necessity. While I kept my car, I mostly relied on the bus or my bike since parking and gas were expensive. Dining out became a fond memory as I convinced my friends that potlucks were the cool new trend. During this, I found some comfort in knowing I could always change my mind. I had solid contacts and a track record of success in my previous roles, so I could potentially rebuild my former career. In the end, while my revamped lifestyle was far from ideal, it was temporary, and well worth it.

Maybe you're the boss. You've worked hard to attain the corner office and a staff you lead and nurture. You enjoy the autonomy to make decisions and set strategy, and find security in knowing you're competent at it. But you *hate* your job, and constantly fantasize about being in a different function, doing something new. Are you willing to trade control and comfort, perhaps just temporarily, for excitement and career satisfaction? It might mean working for someone junior to you, having to perform menial tasks again, or clocking in when you're used to coming and going at will. It will also mean proving yourself and likely making mistakes as you're learning, which can be tough things to swallow. These might be small sacrifices in order to climb the *right* ladder, versus continuing upward on the wrong one.

In addition to looking for creative solutions, also spend time carefully thinking through whether you can take on the practicalities. Maybe you have two small children and an employed spouse, and your desired employer requires a longer commute. Or maybe your target profession initially involves several weeks of travel. During the next few days, realistically assess how family life may be impacted. Maybe you'll be unable to make Tuesday night basketball games and you would need to hire someone to do the yardwork for a while. Balance these sacrifices against the *benefits* your family would realize if you made a successful career switch. Would free time be more enjoyable because you're happier in your job? Could you give up the marathon working weekends and take the kids to the beach instead? Would it allow your family to save more money in the long run?

If you've taken a hard look at your life and just can't budge on that one non-negotiable, then maybe your reservations are real and a career switch isn't for you *right now*. That's okay! You now understand the obstacles and can revisit the decision in a few years.

What is the *value* of true job satisfaction, a sense of accomplishment, or the fulfillment of a dream? The answer will differ for everyone. You need to decide what "worth it" looks like to you.

Decision Versus Action (Don't Confuse These)

Responsibility—Reality—Risk—Resilience

HAVE YOU EVER ATTENDED a work meeting where a big decision was finally made, only to find that in the upcoming weeks nothing changed, and in the next meeting you were back to discussing the same problem? The mere *act* of making a decision feels good, but it can be deceiving. The human brain may interpret the *decision* as the end of the work ("Whew, glad that's done!"), when in fact, *deciding* usually means the work is only just *beginning*. Barry Schwartz, author of *The Paradox of Choice: Why More Is Less*, points out that just thinking about choices is exhausting, and the more options, the worse it is.[1] So, it makes sense that deciding feels good.

And yet, career switching requires *action*. Tony Robbins summed it up nicely when he said, "A real decision is measured by the fact that you've taken new action. If there's no action, you haven't truly decided."[2] In fact, effective change requires many small actions performed consistently over time. Here, our brain once again works against us. There's a part of the brain that thrives on habit as a survival mechanism, which originally kept us safe in unknown territory. In modern society, where we face fewer threats than our caveman ancestors, we need to actively fight our established habits to change. Here are a few strategies successful Switchers deploy to make change happen.

- **One change at a time.** Trying to incorporate several changes at once can overwhelm you. Before you know it, all your changes have failed. If you're switching careers, now isn't the time to buy a new home or start a family.

- **Weave it in.** The less you interrupt other areas of your life, the more a new activity will stick. As you begin your job search, incorporate networking into already scheduled activities like time at the gym, weekly religious services, or your child's soccer games.

- **Get help.** Engage an accountability coach. Social support facilitates change. Identify your resources, including family, and how they might assist with your switch.

As you prepare to make a career switch, feel good about the decision and then *take action* to make it happen.

The Switcher's Top Five Job Search Killers

If you're still reading this, then you've looked at your life and decided there's no room for regret. You're motivated to do what it takes to live life on *your* terms. Good for you! *This is your time.* Before I share the strategies I have seen work for numerous career Switchers, I'm going to alert you to the five biggest mistakes unsuccessful career Switchers make (which I wish I knew when making my first switch!). When you're aware of these missteps, it's easy to avoid them.

SWITCH KILLER #1
Relying on Traditional Job Search Advice

The wisdom you'll find in most career books just won't work for a Switcher. Why? Because the competition you face isn't ordinary. Traditional career books emphasize the importance of using keywords on a resume so that you're selected by applicant tracking systems (ATS) for an interview after applying online. For career Switchers, applying online isn't typically an option and you may not have the right keywords in your resume's previous experience. You must begin with rebranding, not just as far as a resume goes, but extending to every aspect of your professional identity.

Most job search experts recommend networking, and for Switchers it's *absolutely essential*. You need to network into an organization and then convince the hirer to pass up traditional candidates and roll the dice on you. You won't be up for that challenge unless you possess a whole new bag of networking tricks.

What about the interview? Even traditional candidates are nervous about relaying their qualifications. Imagine how it feels to walk into an interview knowing you don't have the expected background. Additionally, Switchers need to get past the hirer's biases and assumptions. No matter how talented or credentialed you are, job seekers with a traditional background in the industry or function will speak the lingo, require less ramp-up time, and know what they're getting into. Switchers seem inherently risky to hirers, as they have a steeper learning curve and may need more hand-holding to get up to speed. Everything you do as a career Switcher needs to account for this reality, and common job search advice doesn't acknowledge it.

SWITCH KILLER #2
Treating a Degree or Certification as a Magic Bullet

The first question I usually hear from Switchers is "Should I return to school?" Unless you're switching to a field like nursing or law, which require specific degrees and licensing, the answer is almost always no. It shouldn't be a *first* step. Many overestimate the value of graduate degrees when it comes to switching careers. Obtaining an MBA or another impressive degree is only the cost of entry. While people will pay attention to you and it will expand your network, you still need to prove you are worth the risk. Think about it: If you had an open role on your team, would you go for a person with the prescribed background in the function or industry or someone who took a few graduate-level classes?

If you attend graduate school as a career-shift strategy, you'll still have a tough job search afterward, *plus* you'll have student-loan debt. Depending on your target, it may be better to volunteer on a project at your current company or create an internship. This will earn points with a potential hiring manager since you'll have applied experience. It will also give you the opportunity to try out the new professional identity before you dive into it. A client, Nancy, earned a master's degree in speech therapy, only to decide she didn't want to work in that field. When she came to me for coaching, she was still undecided on her target career and out $38,000 in loans.

It could be a plus to go back to school. But don't research universities until you perform your due diligence. Assess the actual return on investment that your valuable time and money will earn. I'll go more deeply into deciding whether to go back to school in Chapter Four. If you're already enrolled in a degree program, great! Then, start applying the strategies in this book early. You will have some advantages, like access to a new network through your classmates, but that doesn't mean you can skip steps and expect to land your switch.

SWITCH KILLER #3
Ignoring Your Network

There are very few things in life we can accomplish alone. A career switch is a major goal, and you will only succeed if you activate your network. Many highly accomplished executives shy away from networking when making a career switch. Why neglect such an obvious step? Some haven't searched for a job since college and think applying online is still the standard way to find employment. Others don't know how to mobilize their networks. Small talk and large crowds aren't their thing, so they decide to leave networking to those who are naturally good at it. Many don't network because they feel out of their element, maybe a bit vulnerable, due to their lack of direct experience in the new field. Suddenly, their credentials pale in comparison to junior employees in the industry.

Dean was an executive at a hospital who continued to apply online despite having access to incredible contacts. Dean didn't believe in asking for help; he prided himself on being able to achieve success on his own and wanted to let his qualifications speak for themselves. While this approach had worked for him in the past, when it came time to make a switch he couldn't understand why what had once worked was now a dead end.

Don't let ego prevent you from asking for help. Chapter Eight details strategies for getting past the common networking hurdles that arise from that naysaying voice in your head.

SWITCH KILLER #4
Failing to Know and Neutralize Your Red Flags

Vikram was a successful Ph.D. in pharma who led clinical trials for new drugs. He excelled at his job and, having reached his early forties, was ready for a different challenge. With his deep industry knowledge, Vikram figured that a functional switch to strategy and business development at his company would be a no-brainer. He was stunned when he was repeatedly told that clinical types didn't have a place on the corporate side. Undeterred, Vikram pursued the opportunities he wanted but the harder he fought, the harder hiring managers on the corporate side pushed back. He continued to promote his Ph.D. and clinical accomplishments to hiring managers who were looking for finance, strategy, and data analytics skills. Vikram had failed to rebrand himself.

Every job seeker raises some red flags for hiring managers. It could be a gap between jobs, a layoff, or too many short stints. Fair or not, hirers look for red flags so they can quickly narrow the list of applicants, and being a Switcher is a major red flag. Even if you gain access through a trusted referral, it's important to anticipate potential objections to your abilities, fit, or motivation that may arise. Have genuine, logical responses ready to go. I'll say much more on how to handle your red flags in Chapters Five, Ten, and Eleven.

SWITCH KILLER #5
Disregarding Supply and Demand

Do you remember the Segway, the two-wheeled, stand-up vehicle that some security guards and tour companies still use? The company predicted they would sell 10,000 units per week, but they didn't even reach the 10,000 mark after two years. What happened? Executives failed to identify a market. People didn't have an actual *need* for Segways when they already had bicycles, cars, and—oh, yes—feet!

Assessing the supply and demand for your target job is critical, but even non-Switchers sometimes skip this step. I have many clients who want prestigious roles at companies like Google, overlooking the reality that Google receives over 4,000 resumes per week and hires *one-tenth of 1 percent* of all applicants. More and more executives seek to move from mid- or senior-level operational and engineering roles into sexy finance roles at venture capital (VC) firms. This is among the most challenging double-switches, since VC jobs are so coveted, rarely advertised, and favor candidates with expected career credentials. While a few unicorns manage this switch, they are extremely well-connected and persistent—sometimes pursuing a position for several years, launching their own startup, rubbing elbows with VCs once established, and then eventually transitioning. While this is an extensive process, with no guaranteed outcome, if you want it badly enough and have the talent, contacts, and luck, you can make this switch happen.

Don't make the mistake of neglecting to research the market before proceeding, especially into an unfamiliar industry or function. Remember, the further you stray from a traditional career trajectory, the harder it is to switch. So, do your homework and craft realistic goals based on what you learn.

The "Magic" Equation
for Seizing Career Success

So once you avoid the Switch Killers, it's smooth sailing from here, right? Not exactly. The process of switching careers still takes a lot of determined effort. It's like someone who's sick of being single and has been trying for months to find "the one." Everyone's advice seems to be "It'll happen when you stop trying." Now I'm not a dating expert, but I'm pretty sure if you stop trying it's unlikely there will be a wedding in your future. Okay, I know this advice isn't meant to be taken literally. Rather the message is, "When you stop *stressing* about it, you'll create an environment more conducive to making your dream come true."

However, no matter what your dream is, trying very hard—diligently and unwaveringly—is absolutely necessary, yet it's not sufficient. There are no guarantees that working your butt off will yield success. But it's also true that if you don't give 100 percent, you'll fail. In my experience, the magic equation is:

Targeted Career Goal + Hard Work + *Unknown Factor* = Success

The "unknown factor" in this equation is luck, timing, contacts, or something else altogether. You might not find that reassuring because it means your future depends, in part, on something beyond your control. But to succeed, you must both work very hard *and* have faith that the unknown factor will come along if you persist.

Faith is the belief, drive, and even mild delusion that keeps you going when you're not seeing a clear return on the effort you've invested. There are no short cuts. On days when faith in your career switch wavers, remember:

- **Milton Hershey** started three candy companies, all of which failed, before Hershey's chocolate became a household name.
- **Larry Ellison** had to mortgage his house for a line of credit to keep Oracle afloat.
- **Tim Ferris**'s book *The 4-Hour Workweek* was turned down by twenty-five publishers before it became a bestseller.

These individuals succeeded because they lived by faith and gave 100 percent, even in the face of criticism, rejection, and financial loss. None were guaranteed success. In fact, many talented unknowns worked just as hard and never attained their dreams for some reason, perhaps due to bad timing or luck. However, many simply gave up when there was too much ambiguity and no payoff in sight.

You can't expect great rewards without great risks. It's a harsh career reality to face, but it's what separates extraordinary individuals from everyone else, and successful career changers from those who give up. Successful Switchers plow ahead even when there's no guarantee and the odds are against them. They invest big, knowing rewards are proportional to risks, and that playing it safe will stifle their opportunities. They persist and never waver. And they don't heed the naysayers or take criticism personally. As you embark on your career switch, let this be you!

IN SUMMARY

This chapter helped you confirm whether or not you're a Switcher. Now that you know you are one for sure, and you're ready to conquer your non-negotiables and defeat the Switch Killers, it's time to dive full force into this journey! In Chapter Two, I'll share how the brain can be your biggest nemesis along the way. I'll also share some important psychology principles you can engage to convince skeptical hiring managers to take a chance on you.

CHAPTER ONE SWITCH POINTS

→ Traditional job search methods, such as applying for positions online, don't work for Switchers. You need to get creative in your approach.

→ The bigger your switch is (industry, functional, or double switch) and the more non-negotiables you have, the more difficult the job search process will be.

→ There are no guarantees that persistence, sacrifice, and hard work will pay off, but *without* these qualities, you won't achieve your job switch.

→ Deciding to pursue a goal is only the beginning. A successful career change only happens when you take consistent, relevant action.

→ Ignoring your network, disregarding the market, and failing to prepare for red flags are Switch Killers that will derail your efforts.

The Psychology of
the Job Search

(and How to Use It to Your Advantage!)

As a corporate recruiter, I screened applicants and then advanced candidates who were a potential match for the open role. Hiring managers made the final determination as to whether someone received an offer, while I would strive to understand their decisions so I could send them the best applicants for future openings. When I asked for specific reasons why they passed on a candidate, they would often say, "Something about that guy isn't a good fit, but I can't put my finger on what exactly it is." Although companies I worked with tried to follow structured, unbiased hiring processes, my time as a recruiter taught me that no such thing exists. Hirers are human, so hiring decisions just aren't that scientific. That's good news for a Switcher. (More on this later.)

At every step on your path to a career change, the human brain is playing a part. It's not just *your* brain, it's also the brains of everyone in your network, the hiring managers judging your resume in six seconds, and the employees involved in your interview. Every player is making decisions and taking actions often without fully understanding the deeper, subconscious reasons behind them.

By learning about the psychology of a job search, you'll know how to spot tricks your brain plays on you, and what to do to override them. You'll be armed and ready for doubts and objections in the minds of everyone who evaluates your nontraditional resume, and you can turn those objections to your advantage. In this chapter, I'll give you the inside scoop on *both sides* of the hiring table. As you move through this chapter, you'll learn:

- How your brain is resistant to change, and how to train it to be more adaptable
- How your ego might be getting in the way of your dreams
- What loss aversion is and how to beat it
- What's going on in the mind of the person on the other side of the desk
- The mental characteristics of successful Switchers

Defining the Key Players

Before we move forward, I want to define the roles in the hiring process as I use them in this book. A "recruiter" is an internal employee at the hiring organization whose primary role is to post jobs, source candidates, review resumes, conduct preliminary interviews or phone screens, and pass along qualified applicants to the decision maker. The "hiring manager" is the person in the organization you will be working for if offered the job. This person's primary day-to-day function is something other than hiring (e.g., Accounting Director, VP of Operations, Information Systems Manager) and he is the main decider in the hiring process. A "headhunter" is independent of the hiring organization and is paid to source qualified external candidates. Headhunters' fees are paid by the hiring organization and they are usually engaged to fill senior-level, confidential, or specialty roles for which there is limited availability of qualified applicants.

Humans and Change
(Biology Is Working Against You)

The human brain is amazingly advanced in many ways, but it's also incredibly outdated in other ways. Many of the functions that were designed to protect the survival of our species in the caveman days, for better or worse, still influence our behavior today. Before I launch into what this means for your switch, consider these conditions at work within you.

The human mind has functions that allow us to engage in daily habits without much thought. Our implicit memory enables us to effectively drive a car while listening to music on the radio. We can remember the words to popular songs, and don't need to consciously think about the tasks of driving. If a new cue catches our attention, like a sudden change in road conditions or a ringing cell phone, our brain quickly shifts to focus on the novel stimulus. We easily snap out of our trance and focus our attention back on the present moment. It's a pretty amazing ability.

While the brain's propensity toward habit makes us incredibly efficient, it also hinders our ability to change. Our brain is preprogrammed to continue doing what it's used to doing. So when we're making a career change, we need to fight against our biological instinct to stay in our groove.

In addition to resisting change, the human brain has a bias toward negativity. Humans once survived through an ability to continuously scan for danger in the environment and quickly detect threats. As Neil Pasricha points out, for 99 percent of the human species' existence on this earth "life was short, brutal, and highly competitive, and we have the same brains now that we've had throughout history."[1] Although we no longer need to be on alert for predators, our brain is behind the development curve and still focused on survival. Psychologists have watched this play out time and again. These are the tendencies that could adversely impact your switch.

- The brain typically detects negative information more quickly than positive or neutral information.
- Negative events are flagged and stored for quick access while positive and neutral events fade away more easily.
- People work harder to avoid a loss than to acquire a comparable gain.
- In relationships, it takes five positive interactions to overcome the effects of just one negative interaction.[2]

These tendencies undermine our sense of security, creating an anxious mindset that gets in the way of change. In a job search, this usually takes the form of self-doubt. We ask: "What if I can't do the job?" "What if the team doesn't like me?" "What if I make the wrong choice?" "What if I fail?" This keeps us in a state of mild anxiety and robs us of our ability to muster the courage and energy to change.

Leap!

Responsibility—Reality—*Risk*—Resilience

TO PERSUADE A BABY bird to leap from the nest takes a lot of coaxing, withholding food, and creative methods. Once they do, they realize their full potential and their world is forever changed. Can you imagine the life of a bird that never learned to fly? Humans pursuing their dreams aren't so different from birds leaping into flight. Yet we aren't often coaxed and prodded to realize our full potential. The security of the "nest"—which comes as familiar routines, lifelong habits, perceived obligations, and the comfort of a steady paycheck—is extremely seductive. Without someone relentlessly encouraging you to fly, you're going to need to find the courage to take the leap on your own.

When you feel discouraged in your job switch and you're thinking about giving up, it helps to have your tool kit prepared.

Here are some of the messages that have inspired me when I've tripped over doubt.

→ Mind your thoughts. Your brain believes everything you say and follows suit.

→ A year from now, you'll wish you had started today.

→ You're always one decision away from a completely different life.

→ In the words of Frederick Wilcox, "You can't steal second base and keep one foot on first."[3]

→ Second base, here you come!

Untrain Your Brain

The great news is that our brain is malleable. Just like our muscles, the neural connections that we engage most often grow stronger. So we can practice recognizing and dwelling on the positive to overcome deeply ingrained habits. It isn't easy: It takes awareness, commitment, and repetition to rewire our brains. But it's the first step to making a successful career switch.

As fully mature adults, we're still able to learn and take risks—however, we often use our reasoning skills to argue our opinions instead of to consider unique ideas. Our sense of self-regulation inhibits our willingness to take a chance on something that is unfamiliar or uncomfortable. And our affinity for logic and planning prevents us from seeing innovative solutions to our problems. Yes, our executive functions keep us out of danger and help us make safe decisions, but many of us over-rely on them as an excuse for avoiding novel experiences like a career switch.

To be completely open to learning, we need to be a little vulnerable and let go of the (often false) sense of control we've become accustomed to as adults. The goal isn't to be reckless, but rather to be less concerned about looking silly or failing—obstacles that hold us back from taking reasonable risks. When we're very young, trial and error is a way of life. If something goes wrong, we simply try a different approach, not worrying as much about the longer-term consequences. As adults, we need to be careful not to become zombies to our habits. It's easy to get stuck in "analysis paralysis," in which our thinking convinces us not to grow. And we can shy away from new situations rather than risk damaging our ego. Zen Buddhist monk Shunryu Suzuki taught that "in the beginner's mind there are many possibilities, but in the expert's mind there are few."[4] Although life experience certainly increases our knowledge, it can also cause us to forget that there are infinite perspectives and ideas. The moment we become unwilling to utter the words "I don't know," we lose our potential to grow.

As you embark on your career switch, stay open to when you can consciously take risks. Would it really be such a blow to let go of the reputation you've built and become an unknown in a new field? Are you truly constrained to your hometown, or is your dream career worth relocating for a few years? Will you be a failure if you don't succeed—or could you succeed purely through your courage to try?

SWITCH ACTION

Stretch Out of Your Comfort Zone

HERE'S A SIMPLE EXERCISE to bulk up your risk-taking muscles and strengthen neural connections in the brain that you'll need to break old habits that no longer serve you. For the next thirty days, do something new *each day* that falls outside your comfort zone or natural habits. For example, speak up during staff meetings or, if you tend to be the first to jump into discussions, wait to hear what others have to say. Sign up for a hot yoga class and be willing to feel uncoordinated at first. Go to a movie by yourself or order something from the menu that's unfamiliar. Take a new route to work, watch a competing news channel, sit in a different seat at the dinner table, or brush your teeth with your nondominant hand. The more you S-T-R-E-T-C-H your comfort zone, the more you'll strengthen the neural networks in your brain associated with taking chances and trying novel things, raising the bar on what you find comfortable in future situations.

The Identity Crisis of the Switcher

When Americans meet someone new, the first question they typically ask is, "So, what do you do?" We're programmed to respond to this question automatically: "I'm a lawyer (or programmer or hospital administrator)." Or if you are employed by a well-known organization, you might respond, "I work at Disney." Even though we all fill many roles—parent, soccer coach, pianist, homeowner, spouse—we describe ourselves by what we do for a living, perhaps because we spend most of our waking hours at work. It's also easy, relatable, and culturally appropriate to introduce ourselves in this manner. And over time, our work becomes our identity.

Herminia Ibarra defined *working identity* as "an amalgam of the kind of work you do, the relationships and organizations that form part of your work life, and the story you tell about why you do what you do and how you arrived at that point."[5] According to Ibarra, changing careers means changing identities, which makes sense given that, in the United States, most professionals define themselves by their jobs. This is why, even when you're ready and excited to make a switch, it can be difficult to let go of the title, prestige, and recognition you've earned in your current profession. And you will need to change the way you introduce yourself. Such massive changes can be frightening.

Ibarra called this transition of identity the "murky middle"—a place of ambiguity and uncertainty in the midst of change. It's hard to feel we are losing something, even if it's something we no longer want. But as William Bridges points out, with every transition something in your life must end.[6] There's a natural grieving process associated with letting go of part of your identity. Ego also causes people to struggle with a pay cut, lower title, or less prestigious career even if the change will ultimately make them happy. It's a tough transition. Many people run from the uncomfortable feelings of letting go, deciding instead that it's safer to stay put and rationalizing that the change doesn't make sense after all. The result? They end up settling for where they are and facing regret. But with the courage to go for it, fantastic things await!

Kenny was burned out by the constant stress of more than twenty-five years of practicing law and logging billable hours long after putting his son to bed each night. He had worked tirelessly to attain a solid reputation, but he longed for a job that didn't require him to bring work home. He often mused about how great it would be to deliver pizzas. His coworkers would chuckle, but Kenny wasn't joking. He worked with a financial planner to get his savings in order, and shocked those colleagues by putting in his notice with the firm. Six months after resigning, Kenny attended a holiday party with them, and they laughed at the lawyer-turned-pizza-delivery man. Kenny handled the teasing like a champ, because he knew how much happier he was at the end of each shift when he could crack open a beer and watch a game while his former colleagues were still logging hours.

The brain perceives a job switch as a loss of identity, and it struggles to maintain the status quo. While our ancient, reptilian brain is built for surviving, not thriving, there's hope in our neocortex. This newer, more recently evolved part of the brain can overcome identity clinging if:

- We're aware of it
- We work for what we want
- We're able to let go of our ego

To become a successful Switcher, stop defining yourself by your job title or by the company you work for, and start describing yourself in terms of the *value you add to your audience*. To start thinking this way, you'll need to understand your strengths (expertise), how you're motivated to apply those strengths (interests), your audience's pain point (market), and the intersection of all three. I'll go into depth on this in Chapter Three.

To Ibarra, we don't have just one "true self"; rather, we have many selves throughout our lifetime. Each is built by past experiences, current circumstances, and future dreams. The best way to embrace identity changes is to *get out of our heads and act* by crafting experiments, shifting connections, taking time to evaluate, and making sense of it all to move forward.

If You're Not Ready to Lose, You're Not Ready to Switch

To change is to lose—and humans hate loss. We hate it so much there's a psychological term for it. *Loss aversion* refers to people's tendency "to feel losses more deeply than gains of the same value."[7] Think about how you'd feel if you received an email from Payroll saying you'd be getting an extra $200 in your paycheck next month. Awesome, right? You might even remember to share the news with your spouse when you got home. Now imagine that email says you'll be *losing* $200 in your next paycheck. Although it's the same amount of money, your fury over losing $200 that's rightfully yours would outweigh, and outlast, your happiness about the $200 gain you weren't counting on anyway. Chances are you'd still be griping about it to your spouse weeks later.

We're unknowingly influenced by loss aversion in our decision-making every day. Marketers commonly use scarcity tactics ("Sale: Today Only!" or "Limited Availability!") to convince buyers they'll *miss out* if they don't act now. This concept is also what makes it so difficult to cut our losses at the blackjack table or walk away from a relationship that isn't right for us. We hate to lose the time, money, and energy we've already invested to start over. And it's why we begin to second-guess our choice when making a major career switch. We don't want to lose what we've already invested to get where we are in our career.

Raj was an executive MBA student with a stellar set of accomplishments as a structural engineer. He became interested in pursuing a career in strategy consulting at one of the top firms. Although initially disillusioned when he learned that earning the degree would not be enough to land him the role, he quickly built a network that helped him take the next steps. Raj learned that the role required 80 percent travel, which was more than he was interested in with a young family at home. Disappointed, but not dissuaded, he pressed on and got an interview. Even with his stellar experience and record of achievements, Raj was told he would need to start at an entry-level position like all employees who were new to the firm, which meant reporting to someone ten years his junior and taking a salary hit. Disenchanted at this point, Raj decided to pursue a different path.

When I coach Switchers, they usually start the conversation showing a lot of energy and enthusiasm for their new career path. However, when we move to mapping out the actual steps they'll need to take to make their dream reality, loss aversion quickly kicks in. Here are some of the forms it takes:

- "I can't invest the time unless there is a guarantee it will pay off."
- "I can't afford to take a major pay cut."
- "It's important to maintain my level as a director or my resume will suffer."
- "I've already paid my dues and don't want to start at the bottom again."

As Dan Ariely pointed out, "We commonly overvalue what we have and consider giving it up to be a loss. Losses are psychologically painful."[8] So, even though you're excited about a career switch, your mind can quickly shift to what you might *lose* versus what you might gain—and your motivation may wane. You may feel loss in these areas when making a career transition: time, money, effort, peers, reputation, relationships. But it's important to remember that loss is a risk in any investment equation.

From an evolutionary perspective, being averse to loss (i.e., a threat in our environment) while maximizing resources is what enabled the human species to survive. It's such a primitive instinct that it is often referred to as the "lizard brain"[9] and remains hardwired, even though most of the threats we face today are not lethal. Loss aversion is a key reason why we hold on so tightly to what we have in the face of change. Even when the change is positive (e.g., the opportunity for a promotion), our minds tend to dwell on the losses (e.g., maybe I'll fail and ruin my reputation)—which can keep us stuck.

SWITCH ACTION

Beat Your Lizard Brain

SO HOW CAN YOU overcome loss aversion and leap confidently into a new career? Consider these tricks to beat your lizard brain.

Brain Trick #1: Be objective. Every change includes gains (pros), losses (cons), and things that stay the same (neutral). Since it's human nature to weight losses more heavily, map out all the pros and cons of your career switch on paper so you can look at them more objectively. For example, you may be heartbroken to *lose* the friendships you've built in your current role, but don't forget you'll likely *gain* new friends and you can always stay in touch with people. When facing the unknown, the brain can stir up drama. Be aware and balance it with healthy doses of reality, perhaps from an insightful friend or career coach.

Brain Trick #2: Separate short-term losses from long-term losses. It may be true that you'll take a salary cut initially, but is that worth staying in a profession you loathe until retirement? That's a long time to be unhappy. Make a list of what you'll be *earning* by taking that salary cut, including the intangibles. Perhaps you'll have your weekends free to restore antique cars again or finally be in town to coach Little League. That's worth a lot.

Brain Trick #3: Challenge your fears. Fear is a powerful emotion and one that all living things have in common. We're designed for self-preservation and it doesn't take much to trip our fear response. After working at one company for his entire career, Ryan was seeking a double switch. He was a capable networker and after two years of diligent searching, Ryan was offered his dream job. Although initially thrilled, Ryan's excitement soon gave way to apprehension. "Will a step down in level make me unmarketable?" (Probably not.) "Given my limited experience, perhaps I'll fail, trash my credibility, and end up homeless?" (Nope, not likely.) *Catastrophizing* is believing something bad will happen and, when it does, it'll be a total calamity. It's a cognitive distortion that can steal dreams. Don't let it. Make a list of your "What ifs" and brainstorm how you can address them. Chances are none will come to pass, but having a plan just in case will significantly ease your mind. Ryan accepted the job, by the way, and is doing fantastic.

Brain Trick #4: Identify your true non-negotiables. There may be some losses you truly can't accept, but for most people, actual non-negotiables are few. Be honest with yourself and creative in your thinking. While you may believe you can't live on $1,000 less per month, chances are you can, *and* be happy. You may not *want* to, but then you need to weigh how important money is compared to the job change. As an exercise, pretend that you really did need to give up your non-negotiable. How would you handle it? Be inventive. You may not love all the options you brainstorm, but I bet you'd figure out a solution if you had no other choice.

Brain Trick #5: Choose to delay gratification over the pain of regret. As the saying goes, "Twenty years from now you will be more disappointed by the things you *didn't* do than by the ones you *did* do." Do some reflecting. If you will look back and wish you had made different career choices, the short-term pain of a few losses may feel completely worthwhile. Only you can decide. In a one-click world of immediate gratification, it can be seductive to "eat the marshmallow" now versus waiting to get the big payoff later (as Stanford's famous marshmallow experiment demon-strated).[10] Imagine yourself twenty years from now if you *don't* make this career switch. What have you lost? What have you gained? How do you feel?

I hope these brain tricks show how loss aversion may be influ-encing your decision about a career switch. It's a powerful force that evolved through thousands of years, but once you under-stand it, you can overcome it!

Read the Hirer's Mind

Up until this point we've been addressing how loss aversion im-pacts you as a career Switcher. Keep in mind that hiring managers are affected by loss aversion, too. The cost of a poor hiring decision can be significant, so you need to convince a hiring manager you're worth rolling the dice on. The good news? If you're being hired by a human, you have an opportunity to influence the outcome. While no one can change the minds of others (changing our own mind is hard enough), having insight into your audience's concerns, pain points, and desires can inform your behavior, which may change the outcome of an interaction. Create a significant advantage by being aware of what's going on in the mind of the person on the other side of the desk, and crafting your messages to address these thoughts.

Loss Aversion

Most people assume that a hirer's primary goal is to choose the best candidate, but initially the hirer is more motivated to *avoid loss*. Research indicates that up to 80 percent of company turnover is due to poor hiring.[11] The cost of a bad hiring decision can be significant, which is a setback for Switchers. Since you'll automatically be perceived as riskier, a hiring manager will tend to go with a safer candidate to avoid risking loss. To put it into perspective:

- The cost of replacing an employee can range from two to seven times his or her salary.[12]
- Hiring and training costs for a new employee can vary from 25 percent to 200 percent of annual compensation.[13]
- Highly paid and greater complexity jobs tend to have even higher turnover costs as a percentage of salary.
- In high complexity roles, top performers are more than two times as productive as average performers.[14]

Hiring managers want employees who can hit the ground running, not ones who will need hand-holding or extra training. They're not interested in your "desire to learn" or "passion for the industry" if you don't have something of concrete value to offer them immediately.

That's not a reason to abandon your search. Just being aware of this gives savvy Switchers a clear advantage. You now understand why standard job search methods work against you and why it's impossible to compete with traditional candidates on resumes alone. So structure your search strategy to address the concerns of your audience, something that every job seeker *should* do, but a Switcher absolutely *must* do. I will continue to provide strategies for doing this throughout the book.

Bias

Carl Jung is credited with saying, "Thinking is difficult, that's why most people judge." The job search process is all about judgment. Employers get hundreds of responses to every job ad, so while candidates are hoping their application will get them selected, what they don't realize is that the initial goal of the employer is to *weed out* unqualified candidates. Selection versus elimination involves two completely different mental processes. Why is that significant? Because as a recruiter is *scanning* for differences, his or her brain's negativity bias and deference to habit kicks in full force. And biases, while unfair, are the recruiter's primary tool for reducing the resume pile.

As a Switcher, you're an easy target to weed out, even if you make it to an interview. Human bias is rooted in biology as a defense mechanism that was meant to protect the survival of our species. So if you apply this list of biases to a family of squirrels, they wouldn't sound so harsh. While you cannot always avoid bias, there are strategies to reduce some of the most common types in the hiring process:

- **In-group bias.** Humans tend to trust people who are most like them versus people who are different. This is one of the most common biases of hirers, and unfortunately accounts for many poor hiring decisions.

  What you can do: As a Switcher, it's to your advantage to become as close to, if not a part of, the inner circle of your new crowd. Getting a referral or introduction from someone on the inside is the best way. Join industry associations, attend conferences, post on industry social media sites, or volunteer for a project at work outside of your department. If you keep showing up, eventually you'll be accepted as one of the crowd. Ever been to a city park where fearless squirrels run right up begging for food? It's a similar idea.

☞ **Confirmation bias.** This is where first impressions can help or hurt you. Humans are quick to label and categorize new things as either a potential threat or trustworthy. Once this determination is made, we hone in on behaviors or evidence that support our initial judgment and dismiss behaviors or evidence that disprove it.

What you can do: If you are initially presented as a nontraditional candidate, the hiring manager's initial judgment will be that you don't have the background to do the job. Then she'll constantly scan for proof that she's right about this conclusion. However, if you are introduced by a trusted referral who sings your praises, the initial perception is in your favor. The hiring manager will focus on things that support your candidacy, while turning the volume down on what negates it.

☞ **Stereotyping.** A stereotype is a generalization of a trait, behavior, or belief based on affiliation with a particular group that has come about due to social conditioning. The brain loves to stereotype because it's an easy way to categorize something new into an already existing paradigm in our mind and presumably reduce ambiguity. Say you learn someone is a vegetarian. You might infer that he lives a healthy lifestyle, belongs to a gym, and loves animals—all based on what you believe you know about vegetarians. All, some, or none of these characteristics may be true. In the hiring process, quick assessments tend to lead to bad choices. A hirer may be tempted to make a swift conclusion about you based on your previous profession. (A former client who was a successful "professor-turned-business data analytics manager" initially couldn't convince hirers to get past the stereotype that she'd be too theoretical for the corporate world.) You need to anticipate this and have a plan to get beyond it.

What you can do: No matter what your target market is, do your research and understand the pain points your audience is facing. Be ready to show how you'll use your transferable skills to implement solutions. Resist the urge to get defensive, and rather show empathy: If you were about to hire a Switcher, you'd likely have similar concerns. Put yourself in the hirer's shoes and think about what *you* would need to hear to get past your bias. Then craft your message accordingly, being careful to speak the "language" of your new audience and to let go of the parts of your old identity that do not align with your new target. See Chapter Five for more on that.

☛ **Ambiguity effect.** Most humans dislike ambiguity, and we try to erase it by making assumptions to fill in what we don't know. From an evolutionary perspective, we're programmed to avoid the unknown in case it represents a threat. As a Switcher, you're essentially an "unknown" to a hiring manager.

What you can do: Make assumptions work in your favor and enter via an introduction from a trusted insider. Although your performance will still be an unknown, if your positive attitude, reliability, intelligence, fit, and general likability are relayed by your referral source and confirmed in the initial meeting with the hiring manager, evidence is working in your favor. The hirer's brain will fill in the unknowns with additional positive assumptions.

Bias is real. It has been ingrained into our biology since the beginning of time and although current awareness has brought us a long way, many well-intentioned people still make biased decisions unconsciously every day. While you can't control bias, awareness and smart strategy can do wonders for influencing an outcome.

Emotions

Emotions play a role in all human decision making. Studies show that people who've experienced damage to the part of the brain that drives emotions are unable to make even simple decisions.[15] Meanwhile, business decisions have become more data-driven. Leaders want to understand themes and patterns to ensure their choices will have positive outcomes. The same is true with the hiring process. In most companies, it consists of a complicated series of steps: detailed applications, background checks, interviews, simulations, reference checks, and more recently social media reviews, video bios, and credit score inquiries. Some employers even ask for transcripts, standardized test scores, personality assessments, and cognitive tests. The rationale is that the more data the hirer has, the less likely he or she is to make a hiring error.

While a positive correlation does exist between gathering valid data and making smart hires, with humans involved in the hiring process there's no getting around the role emotions play in swaying outcomes. Remember the hiring manager who said, "There was just something about that guy . . ." but couldn't put his finger on it? That's emotion! Research shows there are good reasons for us *not* to ignore our intuition or gut feelings because there is a lot of value in it.[16]

What can you do to leverage this fact in your favor? Recognize that while data, credentials, and experience are useful, what a hirer really cares about is this: Will you make her life easier and make her, and the team, look good doing it? It's not enough to have a bunch of skills. You need to *connect* those skills to the outcomes they'll produce on the day-to-day job, which will make the hirer instantly feel relief. For example,

Being a liaison to our vendors in sales and distribution in my marketing role enabled me to learn about the challenges and regulations that make it difficult for companies to expand operations in new territories. As a Program Manager for your eCommerce expansion, I can tap into this experience, as well as my connections, to reduce the red tape that tends to slow down growth into new regions.

Make it *simple* for the hirer to see the connection between the skills you bring and the bottom line for the company. Her gut will interpret that feeling as *relief* because her problems will soon be solved. Her brain translates that into the conclusion "hire this person!" Add a positive attitude and likability, and you're golden!

Most candidates walk into an interview, excitedly rattle off a bunch of impressive skills and achievements, and *expect the hirer to do the work of connecting those skills to the needs of the job.* That in turn, leaves hiring managers feeling overwhelmed as you walk out of the door, because they now must spend time matching your skills with their needs. Instead—do the work for them! Scott was an Air Force pilot who combat-tested F-16 fighter jets while leading his squadron in top-secret missions around the globe. Who wouldn't be impressed? However, most hirers had no idea how his remarkable skills and experiences would translate into being an effective project manager. Scott's experiences in the military more than qualified him; he just needed to connect the dots for interviewers. He could say,

As the leader of a team of forty people, my role was to plan projects (missions) down to the hour, including the budget, resources, and supplies needed to effectively achieve our goal, as well as contingency plans since we were often in global locations where means were sparse. As a project manager in your company, I can engage these skills to mobilize cross-functional teams, partner with subject-matter experts to map the design-to-market life cycle, and build in contingencies to ensure we meet our clients' expectations for on-time delivery.

Don't underestimate the role emotions play in hiring decision making. In the words of the great Maya Angelou, "At the end of the day people won't remember what you said or did, they will remember how you made them feel."[17] Make your interviewer feel excited about what you bring to the company and team by showing her specifically how you'll add value.

Conquer Those Inner Demons!

Hirers aren't the only people with distorted perceptions. We're often our own worst enemies when it comes to the job search. Another favorite saying of mine is, "If that voice in your head were a friend, how long would the friendship last?" I'll revisit a few additional mental characteristics that will help you defeat your brain's attempts to thwart your career change efforts. When doubt and fear creep in, that little voice inside our head can be downright mean. And worse, we tend to believe it, even though we have no solid or consistent evidence that these messages are true.

- You're not ready.
- You'll look silly.
- Are you crazy?
- That is dumb.
- You're not worth that much.

The list goes on. Take a major risk, and your lizard brain defenses will kick in to try to "save you" from yourself. From an evolutionary perspective, change is dangerous—but on the other hand, if you can't adapt, you die. Seth Godin wrote: "Fear used to keep our ancestors alive. Fear keeps you from taunting a saber tooth tiger. The thing is, most of us don't have to deal with tigers any longer. But the fear still runs deep. We still feel the same feelings when we face possible failure, but now those feelings revolve around shame. Losing a videogame in private is fine, but asking a stupid question in a meeting is not."[18]

Although our fear is trying to keep us safe, in modern society, it mostly serves to keep us stuck. Here are the five mental characteristics that are universal among Switchers who attain success.

1. Successful Switchers Have a Growth Mindset

Psychologist Carol S. Dweck defined a "growth mindset" as one where individuals believe that hard work and persistence can be engaged to enhance their abilities.[19] Like people with an internal locus of control, they learn from feedback and believe that if they choose different behaviors, they will get different results. Individuals with a growth mindset take responsibility for their actions, and when they make a mistake or something doesn't work as planned, they evaluate the situation and amend for next time.

People with a fixed mindset tend to believe their abilities are static or innate and that practice or greater effort won't make much difference. To maintain this belief, fixed mindset individuals have a desire to look competent, so they believe that failure is not an option. This leads to the avoidance of taking risks, seeking feedback, or trying new things, which means they give up more easily and usually fail to reach their full potential. Going through life with this mindset makes it taxing to accomplish anything, because it renders you powerless.

When making a career switch, you will inevitably make mistakes. You'll screw up, get rejected, and learn the hard way. Making a career switch takes what Angela Duckworth calls "grit," that winning combination of passion and perseverance.[20] If you are unwilling to trip up and embrace growth, you won't get very far.

2. Successful Switchers Don't Compare Themselves to Others

Self-comparison is one of the most common cognitive distortions, and one that causes much misery. Whether it's body image, wealth, or another status symbol, marketers are constantly eliciting our fear of not being enough to get us to use their products or services. When we're attempting something new, we compare ourselves with the pros. We study their techniques, follow their suggestions, and model their actions. While this is a smart way to learn, it can also be demotivating if you start to compare your clumsy beginnings to their hard-earned competence. Don't psych yourself out early in the process. Remember, just as we can always find someone who is better than us at something, we can also find someone who is worse. It all depends on what we search for.

3. Successful Switchers Are Comfortable with Shades of Gray

All-or-nothing attitudes are damaging in the job search process. Sure, it'd be great if someone gave you a shot at a completely new career and let you keep your salary, earned vacation days, and the status perks you've built in your previous profession. But that's unlikely, and if you're thinking, "I want it all or it's not worth it," a major career switch may not be for you. There are no absolutes. No process works every time in every situation. One size does not fit all and there is no magic formula for success that doesn't include some unknown factor (see Chapter One). Knowledge is learning the strategy. Wisdom is applying it correctly.

4. Successful Switchers Don't Fall Prey to the Fallacy of Fairness

Life is not fair. Really, it isn't. It's biased. The more energy you put into fighting for fairness, the less you'll have for making a career switch, as Chapter Eleven will discuss. Is it fair that your dream company hired the traditional/younger/internal candidate? Is it fair that you've been putting your blood, sweat, and tears into this career change and it still hasn't happened? Nope, not at all. But, it's life. Stop pursuing "fair" and start figuring out how to succeed within the boundaries of reality. I once had a boss who worked very hard to treat everyone on the team "fairly." Despite varying levels of competence, effort, and tenure, everyone had to adhere to the same standards and rules for the sheer reason of maintaining "fairness." Guess what? The entire team thought *this* was unfair (especially the ones who had more tenure or felt they were top performers) and the strategy backfired. Fairness is in the eye of the beholder. It's also like a mirage in the desert. Use your time for more fruitful pursuits.

5. Successful Switchers Are Agile

To adapt is to survive and, like most worthwhile endeavors, a career switch rarely happens overnight. Being agile means evaluating the process, seeking feedback, making changes when needed, and above all staying positive in the face of adversity. You will be rejected. You will be disappointed. You may feel like giving up. Expect these feelings going in, create a strategy for dealing with them when they arise, and add them to your checklist as another to-do of being a Switcher.

Jia Jiang, author of *Rejection Proof,* recommends reframing rejection and using it as your motivation.[21] In fact, Jia made a career out of being rejected and set a goal to be rejected for a hundred days straight as a way of desensitizing himself to the sting of rejection.

Do you know what happened? He actually *failed* to get rejected in most cases, leading him to convince a bank to let him make paper airplanes from $100 bills, race bikes at Toys"R"Us, and fly a gyro plane among other crazy stunts!

One of the key transferable skills for Switchers is an ability to be agile, so dig deep and engage this skill. Also, learn when to alter your approach and when to stick with it. This is tough to discern at times. When a strategy isn't working, some people jump to amend it too quickly, before even giving it a chance to start showing benefit. Others hold onto a useless tactic for far too long, afraid to cut their losses and try something different. If you get similar advice from several different people—for instance, if they say you need to get certified before employers will consider you—then it's likely something to pay attention to and address. On the flip side, everyone will have an opinion—so be careful not to change your strategy with every piece of feedback. Follow the data, but also trust your intuition.

IN SUMMARY

When I struggle with what to do next, here's a (slightly gloomy) analogy that always gives me courage and confidence to move forward. Imagine this: If you learned a beloved family member had a fatal disease, but that a cure existed somewhere in the world, how would you go about finding it? Although you had no idea where to even begin searching, who to talk to, or even what to ask, I have no doubt you'd find a way. Never underestimate determination and the will to overcome fear and ambiguity.

On a final note, since loss is a more powerful motivator than gain, if you find your enthusiasm waning, try reframing your job switch as a loss. What will you *lose* if you don't make this change? Years of happiness? A better lifestyle? Seeing your children grow up? You'll face real obstacles in making a switch, so don't let the decoys be what stop you. Find a way.

CHAPTER TWO SWITCH POINTS

→ Your brain wants to keep you safe, but that instinct can get in the way of the courage you need to successfully make a career switch. Don't let it!

→ Loss aversion is a powerful seductress. People feel loss more strongly than gain, so you may be tempted to let things like loss of identity, status, or salary become barriers to your success. Keep top of mind everything you stand to *gain* by making a switch.

→ Hirers are also influenced by loss aversion and will tend to go with the "safe" candidate if you don't assuage their fears about hiring you.

→ Emotions play a role in every human decision. Recognize this and connect the dots between your experience and how it will solve the hiring manager's problems so she feels confident bringing you on board.

→ Bias is a reality in the hiring process, and can be an especially difficult hurdle for Switchers. Learn to identify it and engage strategies to overcome it such as using your network to become an insider.

→ Many of the obstacles Switchers face are self-created. Be aware of falling prey to fallacies such as the illusion of fairness or comparing your progress to others.

SWITCHERS

II

Clarify Your
Plan A

If You Don't Invest, Why Should They?

Figure Out Your Plan A

As a Switcher, you're asking people to make a long-term invest-ment in you. If you can't demonstrate to them that *you've* in-vested in your chosen career, how can you possibly expect them to? Emmy and Golden Globe winner Peter Dinklage, one of the highest paid actors on television, realized the only shot he had of realizing his dream to be a full-time actor was to go all in.

"When I was twenty-nine, I told myself: The next acting job I get, no matter what it pays, I will, from now on, for better or worse, be a working actor. At 29, walking away from data pro-cessing . . . I got a low-paying theatre job in a play called *Imperfect Love*. Which led to other roles, which led to other roles. And I've worked as an actor ever since. Raise the rest of your life to meet you. Don't search for defining moments because they will never come. The moments that define you have already happened . . . . I waited a long time out in the world before I gave myself permission to fail. Please, don't even bother asking, don't bother telling the world you are ready. Show it. Do it."[1]

Before you formally begin your job search, it's important to have a very well-defined target—what I call your "Plan A"—that you can clearly communicate to your network in a way they understand. Showing your network you've done your homework and have thought through the details of a solid Plan A is the only way to prove to them that you're dedicated, serious, determined, and willing to do the work it will take to enter your chosen career. Only then will they fully go to bat for you.

The primary goal of Chapter Three is to make sure your Plan A is precise and thorough, because much of your success depends on aiming for a clear bull's-eye. In this chapter, you will:

- Expand your goals into a fully developed Plan A
- Learn why it's so important to toss Plan B out the window and go all in
- Learn how to translate your skills into your prospective employer's language
- Determine where your expertise, your interests, and the market intersect
- Complete a brainstorming worksheet to clearly define your target
- Understand the role of values in your career switch

Forget Plan B: Why Switchers Need to Put 100 Percent into Plan A

We've already established that making a change, even one you really want, is uncomfortable because your brain is trying to keep you safe in your known habits and away from any danger that might lie in ambiguity ahead. When people feel anxiety, they often cope by creating a Plan B—a backup strategy they can engage if Plan A doesn't work out as they were hoping. Having a backup plan is a great idea in some situations, like when there's an impending blizzard or you're trying a new recipe for a dinner party. But in a job search it can mean a longer transition time or, worse, settling for a role that's not what you want. After all, if you're creating a Plan B, in essence, you *expect* your Plan A to fail.

You have a finite amount of energy, so in a job search you can:

- Focus 100 percent on attaining the job of your dreams, or
- Focus 75 percent on attaining the job of your dreams and 25 percent on attaining a job you'd find acceptable (your safety net).

Why Would You Focus Less than 100 Percent on Your Dreams?

While focusing 100 percent on your dream makes sense on the surface, I can almost hear a "yes, but . . ." coming. "Yes, but I have financial obligations, health reasons, or [insert logical excuse here] so I need a Plan B." This is *fear* kicking in. As so wisely written in the Hindu scripture *The Bhagavad Gita*, "We are kept from our goal not by obstacles, but by a clear path to a lesser goal."[2] You can choose the safe path. And honestly, 25 percent effort might be all that you need to attain your Plan B if it's a traditional path in your field. However, if you go the safe route, you'll find yourself pondering another job search within a few years, or worse, looking back with regret. So, why not focus 100 percent of your energy *now* on what you *really* want to avoid finding yourself back in the same place?

One of the sayings I live by is, "99 percent is a bitch, but 100 percent is a breeze."[3] When you leave *even 1 percent of space* for doubt or second-guessing to creep in, the energy drain on the other 99 percent of your effort can be devastating. Think of it as adding one drop of putrid sewer water to your glass of iced tea. Still want to drink it?

Even the slightest hint of doubt can have a significant negative impact on your success. Research has shown that people with a fallback plan don't work as hard to achieve their goals, and "the mere act of thinking through a backup plan can reduce performance on your primary goal by decreasing your desire for goal achievement." Before even thinking about what to do next, "you might want to wait until you have done everything you can to achieve your primary goal."[4]

Maybe you've weighed this and still can't let go of the idea of a Plan B. Or maybe your spouse or family members are anxious about your career switch and are asking you for a Plan B. It's not unusual for loved ones to feel uneasy, especially because they have little control or influence over the outcome. If that's the case, before redirecting any of your 100 percent to a Plan B, consider the following:

☞ You probably already have an inherent Plan B, even if you're not putting any energy toward it. As a professional, you've built transferable skills that will likely ensure you'll be able to earn a paycheck. And if you maintain a strong network, you're already halfway to most jobs in your current field.

☞ If you must, pursue Plan B *sequentially*, not concurrently. Have a time frame set in your mind when you'll go after Plan A with everything you've got. Maybe you could commit to focusing 100 percent on Plan A for one year, and try everything possible to attain your goal. This way, in the unlikely event you come to a dead end or run out of resources, you'll have a specific date to shift your focus to Plan B.

☞ A Plan B just serves to calm the anxiety that your brain is inflicting on you to protect you from the unknown. Instead, have faith in your ability to achieve Plan A—because if you're not confident in yourself, why should your network be confident in you? Confidence breeds confidence, in yourself and others. You *will* land on your feet and likely have before, so remind yourself and your family of this fact often.

There are no guarantees of success if you go in 100 percent. However, there is a *high* likelihood of failure if you go in at less. At this point, you might be thinking, "Okay, but what if I've identified *two* Plan A's?" Well, then *neither* is really your Plan A and you need to dig deeper to clarify your true target. As Confucius teaches us, "If you chase two rabbits, both will escape." Now is not the time to hedge your bets. Go all in or you may never know what's possible. Do your homework and have faith in your abilities. You'll get much further, much faster if you give 100 percent.

Don't Undervalue Your Values

Responsibility—*Reality*—Risk—Resilience

VALUES CAN BE DESCRIBED as beliefs that are important to us or principles that drive how we choose to live. They are guideposts that tell us what is most meaningful to us.[5] We all have a unique set of values; yours might include family, independence, power, altruism, achievement, learning, health, financial gain, security, or something altogether different. If you haven't put any thought yet into how your dream career path fits with your values, pause and consider it.

Sam absolutely loved his job. He was a doting father of three young children and enjoyed spending downtime with his family and friends in a community where he and his wife had lived all their lives. Sam was offered an opportunity to relocate out of the country for two years to help plan the next Summer Olympics. For Sam, it was a dream role. Except he would need to temporarily leave his family, since he didn't want to uproot his children for such a short time. Sam deeply valued family and community, but also valued career achievement and financial benefits. The position with the Olympic Committee was lucrative, exciting, and would open many doors, but would take him away from everything he loved. Sam had a tough choice to make.

When we build a life that fits well with our chosen values, we're happier. When we don't, we're miserable. Yes, it's possible to put off living your values for a defined period of time. For example, if you're working while attending graduate school in the evenings, you'll have less time to spend with family or get to the gym. But there must be a valid reason and an end in sight, or you'll get burned out.

The simplest way to discover what *you* value most is to examine where you spend your time. If something is important, we find ways to work it into our lives. If health is a value, you probably manage to include exercise, a balanced diet, and decent sleep into your routine. If you place a high value on family, you likely make it home for dinner regularly, spend weekends at soccer tournaments, and find time for family gatherings.

If you believe something is a value and you're *not* making time for it, one of two things is going on: 1) Your life is disconnected from that value and you'll soon burn out if something doesn't change, or 2) it isn't a true value for you. Many people believe they *should* value certain things when the truth is that other things are just more important. Don't judge yourself. If wealth, status, fame, adventure, or autonomy are most important to you, then make time for them. You can't trick yourself into believing you value something that you don't, nor should you. Your sense of disconnect from something you value might have started your new career search to begin with.

You Can't Dual Brand
(So Really, Forget Plan B)

In addition to confidence, agility, and drive, an essential tool in your career Switcher's toolbox is your network. You'll rely heavily on your contacts to open doors for you. Therefore, you can't dual-brand yourself. If you try to pursue two different career paths simultaneously (e.g., your dream and a safety net), your network will become confused and perceive you as fickle or uncertain of what you really want. Then there's little chance they will put you in front of their own valuable network since it could reflect poorly on them. Remember, confidence breeds confidence.

Erik was hell bent on a job in consulting. He thought it would be exciting to travel, work with a creative team, and interact with a variety of clients. I told him that I'd be happy to introduce him to people I know. After a few weeks, Erik asked to be introduced to someone in my network in *marketing* because he heard about data analytics at a conference and thought it would be a more realistic career path. Whoa, what happened to consulting? When he waffled, I wasn't inclined to introduce him to my marketing *or* consulting contacts.

Now may be a fitting time to pause and ask yourself how certain you are about the career path you've chosen for your switch. If you selected it based on anything other than in-depth self-reflection and research including conversations with people in the field, job shadowing, internships, volunteering in the industry, and diligent online market research, you may want to reassess before moving forward. A prestigious title, the potential to make a financial killing, an exotic geographic location, or a beloved hobby don't always equate to your dream day-to-day job. Don't waste your networking efforts on an assumption. Do your homework and be certain. Figure out your Plan A.

The Intersection Where It All Happens

Most people begin figuring out their next career move by looking at the common ground among their interests, their expertise, and the market. You've likely thought this through before picking up this book, but I want to emphasize it from the Switcher's point of view.

Interests

As someone with significant work experience, you can readily assess the tasks you enjoy doing and the ones you don't. You might call the ones you enjoy a "passion" or "purpose." Yes, it's important to job satisfaction to feel motivated, but those terms have a strong connotation and tend to put undue pressure on job seekers.

You might think as a career coach I tell people, "follow your passion," every day. But you'd be wrong. For career changers, "follow your passion" is risky advice, because it usually causes enormous stress. It narrows the search to just one right option, when in today's market that is far from the norm. Most professionals have several jobs throughout their lives, and more goes into job satisfaction than interesting work, such as colleagues, culture, environment, commute, autonomy, boss, and compensation. Depending on your values and stage in life, some of these factors weigh more heavily than others. *You likely have many passions, and they can shift over time.*

Although you've probably heard the Confucius saying, "Find a job you love and you'll never work a day in your life," this isn't true for everyone. Sometimes your passion—whether it's cooking, investing, writing, or traveling—becomes a chore once it's your primary source of income. What used to be a "want to" now feels like a "have to," and where you used to find joy, you now experience pressure. *Sometimes your passion is best left as a hobby.*

While "follow your passion" is a great motto for life, for your career I recommend following your *professional energy*, which will never lead you astray. In the words of Mike Rowe, "Don't follow your passion, but always bring it with you."[6]

SWITCH ACTION

Find Where Your Interests and Expertise Intersect

HERE'S A QUICK WAY to find your professional energy.

- Think about a work accomplishment you're proud of and focus on the parts of the project or situation that truly energized and motivated you. Maybe you loved the camaraderie of working in a collaborative team, the challenge of using your analytic abilities to solve a challenging puzzle, or the buzz of working against the clock to meet a deadline.

- Review a few more accomplishments in this way, and then look for patterns in your energy across all the projects. This can help you refine your next career steps.

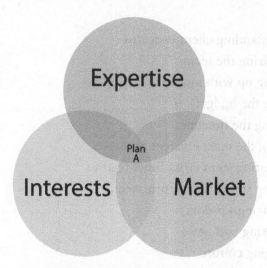

The Intersection Where It All Happens

Expertise

You've gathered a wide array of valuable skills from all the roles you've held, no matter what your titles. To best position yourself as a qualified Switcher, take a closer look at those skills to determine which are marketable and add value to your new employer. Taken together, those marketable skills are your related *expertise*. Your expertise isn't just a list of competencies like "problem solving" or "managing teams." You can begin with these broad terms, but you'll need to go much deeper than the list of words you might find in a job description. It's not enough to tell them you have a skill.

If the company is hiring a consultant and your title has been project manager, to them it's like asking for an apple and getting an orange. Drill down to find overlap in transferable skills utilized by a consultant and a project manager. Break apart your current role and the role you're seeking to their most basic parts. Then find the commonalities between the two. What parts of consulting are you already skilled at from your previous experience in project management? You might be surprised at how much overlap you can find:

- Understanding client concerns
- Mobilizing the team
- Coming up with innovative solutions
- Setting the budget
- Meeting the timeline
- Finding the most efficient processes
- Translating steps cross-functionally
- Keeping stakeholders informed
- Influencing vendors
- Delivering bad news
- Changing culture
- Planning for contingencies

Once you identify the basic ingredients that make up your expertise, reassemble those ingredients to speak to your new audience. Show how you can solve the pain points in their company. It's likely you have more transferable skills than the hirer initially realizes, and *you* need to do the work to spell those skills out for the employer. Get them to look beyond the surface of titles. It's your job to show them that when you boil the roles down to their most basic components, they really aren't so far apart.

Think of it like this: if you start with flour, butter, and eggs, you can add a few more ingredients and whip up some fantastic pancakes. You can also mix in different ingredients to make biscuits or cookies. The foundation hasn't changed, but depending on how you measure and cook the other ingredients, the *outcome* is different. Transferable skills are similar. If you know what result you're aiming for, you can whip up relevant value for your target audience.

Remember, it's 100 percent your responsibility to break down your skills and rebuild them in a way your new audience of network contacts, recruiters, and hiring managers can understand. Otherwise they'll continue to see pancakes when they're looking for cookies.

To identify the skills your new audience wants, look up job descriptions online, ask your network directly, check out profiles on LinkedIn or other professional networking sites, read industry materials, attend conferences, check out association websites—the list goes on.

Making a career switch is a relatively ambiguous, unstructured process. That alone is enough to stall progress. However, don't let this fear of ambiguity derail your efforts. Tap into your resources and problem-solving abilities to create a structure that works for your style.

SWITCH ACTION

Clearly Define Your Skills

REFLECT FOR A MOMENT on the transferable skills you have. In your journal, create a timeline for your career in three- to five-year increments. For each period on your timeline, list the critical skills you gained or strengthened. Include different projects you worked on, significant achievements or responsibilities, any recognition or awards you received, key promotions, training, internships, global experience, certifications, and even volunteer roles.

Next drill down to the *most basic skills* that contributed to your success in these situations, and then circle those most relevant to your *new* career target. For example, if your goal is to switch from an office manager position to a role in event planning, identify the basic skills you possess that overlap with successful event planners such as your ability to work with a diverse set of clients, to coordinate and execute short- and long-term logistics, to establish and manage a budget, and to identify and negotiate with vendors.

The final step is demonstrating how you can solve key concerns in your desired role using these transferable skills. To do this, you will need to know your audience, so read on, we'll get there!

Market

Many job seekers pay close attention to their interests and expertise, but neglect to keep tabs on the market. This is a mistake because there needs to be a customer for what you're selling. For instance, if you want to open a brick-and-mortar bookstore, you might have the interest and experience, but you may not be very successful since online retailers and ebooks have overtaken the market.

There are many ways to research the economy to better understand the market outlook of your chosen path. Follow companies online through social media, read industry publications, pay attention to business news, scan job boards to see who is hiring and for what roles (this is one of the few times I'll advocate for online job boards!), or simply Google the industry. The internet has made this process much simpler. So don't move forward blindly. If there isn't a strong market for your skills, don't automatically abandon your goal. Just understand that a weak or declining outlook will add an obstacle to your path.

SWITCH ACTION

Narrowing Your Target by Networking

IF YOU STILL HAVE unanswered questions or gaps in your Plan A, setting up brief, structured meetings with experts can help you source the additional data. Then you can feel certain of your target. When you network to narrow down your Plan A (vs. networking when ready to dive headfirst into your switch), follow these guidelines:

- **Be strategic about who you ask.** This isn't the time to use your most well-connected or influential contacts. Start with people closest to you: friends, family, neighbors. Think about people who care about you, want you to succeed, and will give you honest feedback. If the people closest to you don't have the perspective you need, consider reaching out to a career coach who can fill in gaps and brainstorm the contacts to move you forward.

- **Avoid asking questions you can find answers to on the internet.** Don't waste someone's time or expect them to do the work for you by asking *"What do you think I should do?"* By doing this, you shirk responsibility. No one else—a spouse, career coach, headhunter, or colleague—has this answer for you. Figuring it out for yourself is part of the process.

- **Have clear goals about what you want to learn in the meeting.** Be organized. Come prepared with specific questions. Have an open mind, but maintain perspective. Everyone is offering advice from his or her experience, which means it isn't completely objective. While it can be helpful to ask for opinions, like *"What surprised you most about working in finance?"* recognize that one person's experience may not be yours. Filter the information accordingly.

Where Interest, Expertise, and the Market Intersect: An Example

Greg built a career as a corporate attorney for a large pharmaceutical company in Boston but wanted to become a product manager for a company in San Francisco that made wearable, technology-based healthcare devices—which is an awesome start on a focused Plan A! When he broke down his skills into basic parts, aligned his interests, and researched the market, his results looked something like this.

INTERESTS

- Managing the user specifications, production timetables, pricing strategy, branding, and go-to-market plan for wearable health-care technology related to diabetes prevention and maintenance.

EXPERTISE (RELATED TO THE PLAN A TARGET)

- Deep experience working cross-functionally to accomplish results
- Strong understanding of the healthcare landscape both domestically and abroad from working in pharma for twelve years
- Ability to negotiate, mediate, and influence win-win solutions without direct authority
- Skilled in understanding and demystifying complex policies and regulations, and finding creative ways to work within guidelines to move business goals forward
- Capable of building strong business relationships with vendors, subcontractors, and suppliers
- Excellent research, analytical, and communication skills, including a reputation for building solid cases for change

- Experience analyzing legal and compliance issues related to proposed products to reduce liability
- Excellent contracting and pricing skills
- Managed a project team to create new initiatives for streamlining legal processes by integrating innovative software solutions
- Natural ability to quickly learn, understand, and train others on new software, including a double major in history and computer science
- Personal experience with the difficulties of managing life with diabetes

MARKET NEEDS

- The market for wearable technologies is growing as the world moves toward being more connected
- Healthcare as an industry has grown with the aging Baby Boomer generation
- Statistics show the need to manage and prevent diabetes is growing

Once you've identified the place where your interests, your expertise, and the market intersect, you'll feel more self-assured about the switch. Now it's time to clarify so that your target makes sense to your network and to the future hiring manager.

Hit the Bull's-Eye: Formulate Your Plan A

Your network holds the key to your career switch, so it's important to give them something they can understand and help you with. The more thoroughly defined your target is, the more energy you'll have spent researching the market, understanding your value at the most intricate levels, and building confidence in your choice. This laser focus will make your job search more effective and prepare you to kick butt in the interview. You'll come across as knowledgeable, focused, and confident no matter what questions are thrown at you.

Creating a solid Plan A takes introspection, research, and analysis. You'll know you have a clear target when you are able to clearly describe the following to your network (a variety of sample answers are in parentheses):

- **Target industry** (pharma, telecommunications, retail)
- **Target function or department** (supply chain, human resources, marketing)
- **Target title or position** (project manager, corporate trainer)
- **Target level** (director, associate, regional manager)
- **Target duties or responsibilities** (manage global software implementation, recruit and interview new talent)
- **Target companies** (Uber, Goldman Sachs, Ernst & Young, Johnson & Johnson, Campbell's Soup)
- **Target geography** (Tri-state region, Greater Denver area, Silicon Valley)
- **Target culture** (cutting-edge startup, promote-from-within culture)
- **Target size** (fewer than 100 people, $100–300 million in annual revenue)
- **Target compensation** (commission-based, full health benefits, base salary of $105,000+)
- **Target pain points you'll solve** (identify and troubleshoot inefficiencies in operational procedure to cut down on loss, manage the company's corporate investments to maximize the bottom line)
- **Target skills you'll use to solve them** (strong ability to create structure from ambiguity, deep knowledge of regulatory practices, unique combination of legal experience and programming expertise)

- **Target network** (my former colleague Art Gruenberg who is now at General Mills, my neighbor Ashish Bhatt who works at Nike)

With this, your Plan A becomes the answer to the question, "What do you want to do?" While a clear target is something every job seeker needs, it's critical to Switchers who must convince their network they've done their homework and are serious about next steps.

Some people worry that by focusing or narrowing their target, they will limit their options. But the opposite is true. When you're clear about what you want, you are perceived as confident and collected. People *want* to help (and hire!) self-assured, poised professionals, and chances are they'll bring you *more* opportunities if you're focused, not fewer. This may sound counterintuitive at first, but think about it. If you were considering connecting someone with your precious contacts, would you rather help if he or she is able to clearly communicate the target and ask you for something specific like "After spending ten months taking online technology courses, and volunteering with local nonprofits to set up their patron databases, I'm confident a full-time career in customer analytics is a great fit for my skills and interests"? Or would you be more likely to help my friend Erik from earlier, who hasn't put much thought into his next step, but thinks it would be "pretty cool" to work at a startup in San Francisco? (This was his next great idea, a few months after the fleeting interest in data analytics.)

Do the work for your network. I promise, it will pay off by creating the ambassadors you'll need to open the doors to the decision makers.

SWITCH ACTION

Your Bull's-Eye Brainstorming Worksheet

ONCE YOU'VE MAPPED OUT your expertise, your interests, and the market, the last step to shoring up your Plan A is to overlay this information with the details of your target job. The Bull's-Eye Brainstorming Worksheet is designed to help you do this. Greg's example worksheet is included here, although ideally yours will be much denser, with twenty or more companies and several network contacts. You can re-create this grid in your journal and write in your own responses. Then use this information to create a summary in a brief paragraph.

CATEGORY	GREG'S TARGET
Industry	Healthcare technology
Function/department	Research & development or marketing
Title/position	Product manager
Level	Manager or team lead
Duties and responsibilities	Research and analyze market needs, oversee design specifications, manage time-tables and budget, guide strategic branding
Companies	Fitbit, Biotricity, Chrono Therapeutics, Health Devices, LLC
Geography	San Francisco/Silicon Valley
Culture	Progressive midsized company or mature startup, growth culture, concerned with social impact
Size	Fewer than 500 employees, growing globally
Compensation	Minimum base of $110k, ideally a merit bonus and relocation allowance

CATEGORY	GREG'S TARGET
Pain points you'll solve	Effectively navigate global regulations that stall the distribution of new products, build customer and vendor base through contacts in healthcare industry
Skills you'll use to solve pain points	Deep knowledge of regulatory practices; unique combination of legal experience, healthcare knowledge, and programming expertise
Network	My wife's family who resides in the San Francisco suburbs; my former colleague who works as a product manager; my alumni network, including Nick Roycroft, Ginger Ryan, Peg Cahill

GREG'S PLAN A SUMMARY: To apply my twelve years of experience in the healthcare industry, specifically in building strong vendor relationships, analyzing complex data, pricing and contracting, and demystifying global policies and regulations, with my technology expertise to build on my passion for managing the development and global distribution of affordable, wearable technology products in the area of diabetes prevention and maintenance to change the landscape of the growing population of individuals suffering with this deadly disease.

IN SUMMARY

Although it may take time to create a solid Plan A, the process is critical to your success as a Switcher. The more you struggle to get specific about your interests, wrestle with your targets, and think through your transferable skills, the better able you'll be to confidently articulate these messages to your new audience. A willingness to do the work of formulating a crisp Plan A is what sets successful job seekers apart from the pack.

CHAPTER THREE SWITCH POINTS

→ Go all in on Plan A! Don't undermine yourself by splitting your energy between two goals.

→ Boil your skills and the skills needed for your target role down into their most basic components so that you can understand the overlap.

→ Take time to map out the intersection of your Interests, your (related) Expertise, and the Market for a solid Plan A. The struggle to reach clarity is vital and will set you up for success in the networking and interview processes.

→ Clearly define your target. Don't fear going too narrow: Most people keep their target too *broad*, which makes it harder for your network to help you, or for a hiring manager to take a chance on you.

→ Completing the Bull's-Eye Brainstorming Worksheet is a helpful way to keep your target clear, precise, and at the front of your mind.

→ Values play a key role in career satisfaction. Take these into account when making decisions related to your switch.

Change Isn't Linear

Mapping Your Path to
a Career Switch

When attempting to summit Mount Everest, climbers can't simply make a beeline to the top. They must climb to each camp at various altitudes and then *descend* again to acclimatize before ascending to the next camp. This up and down process adds time and effort to the task, but an eye fixed on the prize as well as sheer will can keep summiteers going for the two months it takes to reach the top. And only half who attempt to summit Everest succeed.

Few things in life proceed as planned. If you chart any significant project, process, or problem, the steps between one and done look more like random doodles than a straight line. Effectively defining your Plan A sets you off on an awesome start. Clarifying your target causes you to think about several aspects of the switch you may not have considered previously. This helps you map the path to get there.

In this chapter, you will:

- Learn about alternative paths to your career goal
- Weigh the benefits of a direct path to your chosen role in comparison with a more gradual one

- Consider whether returning to school is a wise choice for you
- Learn how to address a career gap with prospective employers
- See how a desire for comfort and instant gratification can thwart your switch

Take the Right Path, Not the Easiest One

Many Switchers go through a few iterations of their Plan A. Shaping and redefining the details as you go is completely normal and, after all, this is a new career. You may have researched it ad nauseam but haven't yet *experienced* it, so there is a lot to still learn. Clarity comes through action including each new person you meet, conversation you have, situation you experience, and article you read. This doesn't mean you should shift course with every new piece of data; simply remain open to novel information and adjust where needed while staying true to your target.

In the previous chapter, we met Greg, the corporate lawyer in a Boston pharmaceutical company who wanted to make a double switch to a product manager in a wearable technology company in San Francisco. As with any double Switcher, Greg has some hurdles ahead of him. He lacks direct experience in areas that would be attractive to a hiring manager in product management such as marketing skills, business development, and direct technology experience (his degree in computer science is helpful, but experience always trumps education). On top of those hurdles, he's added a cross-country relocation to the mix, which introduces another layer of complexity.

Few things are impossible, but unless Greg is incredibly well-connected with a hiring manager at a company he is targeting in San Francisco, he may have a long search in front of him. An option might be to use a stepping stone to improve his chances.

The Stepping Stone Switch

Some double switches are tougher to complete in one fell swoop. For these, you may consider a "stepping stone switch"—taking an interim job on the way to your ultimate career goal. For example, you might get your foot in the door of the new industry since industry changes are the least challenging of all the switch types. If you're currently in a marketing analyst function at a university, but your aim is to be an event planner in hospitality, you might first pursue a marketing position in a hospitality company (step one: industry switch from academia to hospitality). You can prove yourself for two years as a top analyst, while networking internally with the event planning department, and possibly getting involved in planning events on your own time. Then when the opportunity presents itself, pursue a functional switch into your target field within the hospitality company where you've proven your chops as a stellar employee (step two: functional switch to an event planning role). Since your ultimate goal is now two years away, this may initially sound unappealing. But if you've determined this is the right path for your long-term career, two years isn't that long.

If you choose this stepping-stone option, you'll want to research the company culture before accepting an offer. Do they encourage growth from within? Are they supportive of functional switches? If not, you may get pigeonholed into your current role and be unable to successfully complete the double switch.

For Greg, taking a cross-country move out of the mix may be a helpful stepping-stone strategy if he can find suitable employees in Boston. Geographic relocations add a layer of risk that hirers tend to avoid. In addition to the expense (if they offer a relocation allowance), hirers are concerned a candidate will have a change of heart or perhaps accompanying family members won't adjust to the new location. It happens. A tangible reason for the relocation, such as wanting to be closer to extended family in the new city or having lived there in the past can allay a hirer's concerns, but may ultimately not be enough to sway them if you're also making a career switch.

It can be difficult to assess if a Stepping Stone Switch is the right path to take. Here are some things to consider:

☞ **Don't automatically assume a Stepping Stone Switch is your only option.** Switchers can sell themselves short by convincing themselves this is the only way to make a double switch. Sometimes you just need to do more research or networking. Or perhaps closing a certain skill gap (e.g., managing a budget, gaining direct client experience) will be enough to make you competitive for a career change. You may need to start at the bottom, but this may also be more desirable than finding a stepping stone role for a few years.

☞ **Don't rule out the Stepping Stone Switch, either.** This may be a faster way out of your current role and it may help you avoid short-term losses in salary or level. For example, if you don't want to spend another day as an analyst, let alone two more years, you could attempt to move into an event planning position with your *current* employer, and then change industries once you've gotten some experience under your belt (this is a variation of the stepping-stone switch mentioned previously). It's much easier to make a functional switch internally, especially if you work in a mid- to large-sized company, have a track record of doing awesome work, and are well-networked with the department you wish to move into.

☞ **Be creative.** Sometimes you can close a skill gap through volunteer roles, a certification, or a self-created internship. This won't always work and takes some creativity, but depending on your Plan A, it is worth exploring before you firmly decide your only option is a stepping stone route. A doctor I know spent his spare time assisting with an investment deal his hospital was involved in because he wanted a career in finance. For weeks, he came to the office two hours early to participate on the investment project voluntarily. He gained real-world experience in finance and met people in the industry who were so impressed with his motivation and commitment, they invited him to remain involved with the team. In the end, the time sacrificed may be worth it. Experience is experience whether you're paid or not.

☛ **Give yourself a time frame.** If signs point to "go," then try for the direct double switch! After six to eight months of diligent searching, if you continue to hit a brick wall, you can reassess if a Stepping Stone Switch might be a better option for you.

If you need to take a stepping stone path to your new career, don't get discouraged. There are many ways to get from Point A to Point B; some just require a brief detour. You will grow your network and deepen your skills and confidence along the way. This crossroads is when many Switchers throw in the towel and give up. Don't! If you really want it, there's a way. It just may be different than the path you initially imagined. Search for the stepping stone that will ultimately get you where you want to be!

Should I Go Back to School?

When deciding to make a career switch, the first thing many people consider, even before putting deep thought into whether the new path is the *right* one, is "Should I go back to school?" For some career switches, the path is clear cut: If you want to be a dentist or therapist, you'll have to pursue formal education to earn the necessary credentials. For others, there is more to consider: If you want to switch industries or functions (or both) within business, you need to consider the return on investment. Sinking thousands of dollars and possibly years of time into additional education may or may not open the doors you expect it to.

As master rationalizers, we can easily make a case for further education. "An advanced degree will make me more knowledgeable in my new field," you might think, or "It will help me network with people who share my interests, and make me more marketable with potential employers." Yes, that's true. But it will also set you back a few years and paychecks. And, unless you're 100 percent certain you want to build a long-term career in this new field and that an advanced degree is a requirement, going back to school isn't necessarily the best path. What happens in the classroom is often very different than what happens at the office.

Sure, if you want to deepen your knowledge or check a major personal goal off your bucket list, by all means, complete those applications! However, if you believe a degree will automatically make your career switch significantly easier, you may be disappointed.

SWITCH ACTION

Should You Go Back to School?

UNLESS THERE IS SIGNIFICANT data indicating that an additional degree or extensive certification is critical to success in your new career choice (and sometimes there is), before diving into those tedious applications consider these questions:

- **Are you pursuing a degree to make your job search easier?** At the end of your degree, you'll still have a tough job search process waiting for you. The University Career Center may help with a resume and some interview practice, but then you're likely on your own for the bulk of the job search.

- **Does the program offer internships or other real-world projects where you can build hands-on experience?** When you're looking for a job, actual experience will always trump classroom time. If returning to school is necessary, look for programs that support on-the-job experiences. They will help you to gain competitive skills and access to potential employers.

- **Will the debt you incur put you in a challenging financial situation once you finish school?** When considering any investment, you need to plan for the long-term. It may take longer than you think to find a job in your new field or you may be facing a pay cut. Do your due diligence in advance and plan accordingly. Countless applicants make assumptions about what graduate programs offer in terms of job placement, just to be let down in the end. Brochures are meant to pique your interest. Investigate and ask the tough questions.

- **Can you build experience in other ways, like volunteering, self-created internships, or shadowing an expert?** This is less structured and takes some creativity; however, it can be a more financially feasible way to get the actual experience and contacts you need. Many people avoid this option because it is ambiguous, but the road less traveled is often the best path in a switch. Remember the physician from a few pages back who helped with his hospital's financial investment project? That was a self-created internship.

- **Is it possible an advanced degree will make you overqualified for the role you're seeking?** It is not unheard of. Do your research.

Gigs and Portfolios

If given the choice, would you shop at a store where all sales are final or at one with a liberal return policy? The opportunity to change our minds is anxiety-reducing because it means if we make a mistake, it can be undone. Smart retailers understand that "reversible decisions" are inherently less risky for shoppers and therefore easier to justify. So people buy more!

You can use this psychology tactic to your advantage in the workplace. By adding the word "experiment" to a request, you've made it a reversible decision, which is much less risky for your boss. For example, "Working from home one day each week would significantly boost my productivity and satisfaction. Can we experiment with this arrangement for three months?" This tactic can also create a stepping stone career to your dream job. The president of the Society for Human Resource Management noted that the "rise of freelance workers" was one of the five biggest employment trends.[1] A portfolio career essentially means you are earning your income from a variety of sources instead of one full-time job. The "gig economy" is on the rise, and it's not uncommon for individuals to create a portfolio of gigs to earn a living. You can be a restaurant manager on weekends, adjunct science professor on Tuesdays and Thursdays, and custom web designer on demand. The sky's the limit when you engage your creativity.

The reason this employment trend can work for a Switcher is because, with more companies open to contract and part-time work, you may be able to get access to your dream role on an experimental or trial basis. Employers are much more likely to hire a risky candidate for a three-month project since they can easily let you go after ninety days if it doesn't work out. This gives you a chance to prove you can do it!

If finding a paid role doesn't work, you can also try a self-created internship using the reversible decision strategy. Identify a need, put together a proposal, and offer to work for free. While you may need to keep your day job, consider completing the internship on weekends, early in the morning, or by taking a brief leave of absence from your current employer. I've even seen clients use their vacation days or ask if they could work four ten-hour days to free up a weekday for a gig. Award-winning director and producer Steven Spielberg was an intern with Universal Studios when he was a teenager. Although he wasn't permitted access to the studio, he regularly sneaked in to network with directors. He eventually created a short film and the executives were so impressed, Spielberg was offered a seven-year contract.

A self-created internship or short-term gig won't be something you can find online; you'll need to create the role and then convince an employer to permit you to perform it. This is where your network and using the "experiment" terminology will help significantly. If you work in a large company, start there. Who wouldn't want free labor? If not, talk to friends and family. Perhaps they can brainstorm an idea that could work in a company where they are employed. No luck? Look at small businesses, universities, or nonprofits who are typically resource-strapped and may welcome the additional hands. If you really want it, you'll find a way. If not, you'll find an excuse. Make it happen!

A Word on the Absentee Switcher

There are reasons why professionals might voluntarily leave the workforce for several years: to raise a family, to be a caregiver to an ill parent, to follow a spouse's relocation. When it's time to return to your career, you might find the market has changed, your interests have changed, or both. You're excited to rejoin the workforce, but you may discover that employers do not share a similar level of enthusiasm for hiring you. You likely face some of the same challenges as Switchers as you convince an employer to roll the dice on you (see Chapters Five, Ten, and Eleven). Therefore, this is likely not the time to pursue a double switch, unless you're incredibly well-connected to the decision makers, are comfortable starting in a very junior role, or you want to enter a specialized field, such as nursing, that requires a specific degree or certification.

Employers will already be biased against the gap on your resume, so if you have your heart set on making a major switch, you may want to consider using a stepping stone. This method will ensure you're able to reenter the workforce in a timely manner, while also working your way toward your ultimate career goal.

Why You're Not Getting What You *Really* Want

Responsibility—Reality—Risk—Resilience

YOU MIGHT HAVE BEEN dreaming about making a career switch for months or even years before committing to making it happen. And you're not alone. Day after day, we talk about the lofty goals we want to achieve in life—to buy a home, travel the world, or switch careers. Unfortunately, many of us find ourselves talking about the same goals year after year. Most of our goals are completely within our reach, so why aren't we achieving them?

The answer is rooted in psychology: Because we are *choosing* to make our lofty goals *secondary* to a more important (and likely short-term) *primary* goal by the *daily choices we make*. Let me rephrase that. Sizeable goals like a career switch don't just happen. They are attained through a culmination of small, consistent actions that we take toward them every day. If you write for an hour each day, you'll eventually finish the book you've been dreaming of writing. If you wake up early to swim, run, or bike for an hour before work, you'll get in shape to enter a triathlon.

The daily choices we make accumulate to form our life's achievements, and these choices *are always in service of our primary goals.* So, while you may believe saving money for a home is your primary goal, if you continue to succumb to impulse purchases, short-term comfort may be your true primary goal.

The pleasure-seeking brain is a bit of a sucker for instant gratification, and our "one-click" world has only served to reinforce this habit. However, substantial goals such as a career switch require diligence and consistent action over time. And change is rarely linear. Missteps, setbacks, and hurdles can lead to unforeseen detours in even the best-laid plans. This is where most Switchers fall back into comfort rather than persevering in pursuit and service of their primary goal, which is the new job.

When in doubt about what goal you are choosing to serve, just look at your actions.

It's our *actions*, not our thoughts or intentions, that make our dreams a reality.

So, what specifically is getting in the way of what you *truly* want? Habit, immediate gratification, a desire to put others' needs before your own, getting sidetracked by easier pursuits, or an unconscious fear of failure can all be at play. If a stepping stone job is necessary to successfully attain your ultimate career, don't permit these distractions to derail you. Humans are master rationalizers and procrastinators, but once we understand what's getting in the way of achieving what we *really* want, we have the power to change it. Here's how:

In each moment, we face a decision point about how to spend our time—watching a rerun on TV or attending an industry meet-and-greet, sleeping in or using the extra hour in the morning to meet a contact for coffee. When at this fork in the road, pause and ask yourself whether the action you are about to choose will take you *closer* to what you want or *move you away* from it. Then, choose wisely.

IN SUMMARY

Like summiting a mountain, there are many routes to your goal. Some are faster, but more difficult. Others take more time, but may increase your odds. While you're the only one who can determine what path is right for you based on your resources, circumstances, and goals, the fact that there are different paths to choose increases your odds for success.

CHAPTER FOUR SWITCH POINTS

→ Some double Switchers may require a stepping stone career. Depending on the strength of your network, consider if a stepping stone role is a useful strategy.

→ Going back to school might feel like a worthwhile step toward your new career, but remember that a tough job search will still be waiting at the end. Find out if the return on investment is worth it.

→ The rise of the gig economy is creating new opportunities. Don't rule this out as a creative way to make your career switch a reality.

→ Stepping out of the workforce is not unusual. The difficulty of making a switch as you're reintegrating will depend on the length of time you've been away, your profession and skill set, and the strength of your network.

→ We are always serving our primary goal. If you're not getting what you want, chances are you are making comfort or short-term gratification your primary goal, and whatever you *think* is your true goal is your secondary goal.

III

Craft
Your Brand Value
Proposition

(Re)Brand or Be Branded

Craft Your Professional Identity

Okay, so you've figured out your Plan A and how your expertise can help solve your audience's pain points. Nice work! But, is your Plan A what people currently *associate* with you? When your colleagues, network contacts, or others in your professional circle describe you, do they paint a clear picture that aligns with your Plan A? Probably not, because even if you haven't consciously intended to, over time you've been building your "brand" through your actions, associations, roles, social media presence, and professional history. And that brand probably aligns more closely with your *current* profession rather than your new target.

In this chapter, you'll recognize the brand you've built in your career, and take a close look at how well that brand is serving your *new* path as a career Switcher. You will learn:

- What a professional brand is and why it's important
- How to craft a brand for yourself that's authentic and serves you well in your career switch

- How to write a brand statement to help clarify the brand you present to your network
- How to determine your unique selling point and brand value proposition, so you can clearly communicate to hirers why you're the best candidate for the job
- Tips to ensure red flags don't become a part of your brand

What "Brand" Is and Why It Matters

Our brain processes 400 billion bits of information each second (although we're only aware of 2,000 bits), and we need to efficiently filter that information to figure out how and where each piece fits into our world.[1] Learning to organize and label data quickly frees us up to focus on the next piece of input. Over the course of your career, the people you interact with subconsciously notice and catalogue several factors about you through your actions, and then judge and categorize them to determine what becomes your reputation—that is, your brand. This vast array of factors includes:

- Written and spoken interactions (email, comments, feedback)
- Body language and tone (eye rolling, smiling, sarcasm)
- Social media (blogs, photos, "likes")
- Marketing and advertising (LinkedIn, business cards, introduction)
- Associations (teams, friends, groups)
- Appearance (dress, style, grooming)
- Hobbies (activities, causes, interests)
- Environment (office décor, clutter, closed door)
- Actions (responsiveness, timeliness, helpfulness)
- Attitudes (optimism, openness, aggression)
- Worldviews (political, socioeconomic, religious)

Everything you put out into the world adds to the overall picture of your brand, whether you do it consciously or not. Are you the unofficial technology whiz who colleagues seek out when their computers crash? Are you famous for bringing your homemade toffee bars to the office and block parties alike? Are you regularly five minutes late? Is your door always closed? Can you be counted on to be the one who celebrates others' achievements? Do you use social media to broadcast your personal dramas? Are you the person constantly texting at staff meetings? Or the one who is always organizing volunteer outings? Do you have a knack for remembering everyone's name and birthday? Are you the "Debbie Downer" of the team? Or perhaps the first (and last) person at happy hour?

People notice, and taken together, these traits make up how others *experience* you. You cannot pick and choose which behaviors are included in, and which are excluded from, others' perceptions of you. Everything counts and culminates into your brand.

Mel was overlooked for a promotion and was considering leaving her company. While Mel never missed deadlines, typically produced a solid work product, and was generally viewed as competent by external customers, the *way* she completed work left a lot of room for improvement. She took several days to respond to internal emails, was frequently late for staff meetings, and often waited until the eleventh hour to request data, which meant her colleagues had to scramble to produce what she needed. Mel got away with this behavior because she got the job done and was friendly, but her brand became a major obstacle once she wanted a leadership role.

Just because you produce the highest sales numbers at the end of the month, if you leave dead bodies in your wake doing it, your network is taking this into account when determining your overall brand.

SWITCH ACTION

Research Your Brand

TO GET A BETTER sense of what people see as your current brand, try this brief exercise.

Select. Choose ten people to contact. Include people from a variety of circles like friends, family members, and work colleagues.

Ask. Email the people on your list the following questions:

→ What are my strengths?

→ What areas need more development?

→ What am I known for in the group (at work, in your family, in your group of friends)?

Give little other direction. Allow them to write what comes to mind.

Evaluate. When you sift through the responses, what themes and patterns emerge? Do different groups see different things? Do you agree with the feedback? How does it fit (or not) with your Plan A?

Chances are that when you evaluated the responses, you found some alignment and common themes. However, people likely mentioned a mix of personal and professional qualities, so if you really want to hone in on your *career* brand, redo the exercise. This time, focus specifically on your professional strengths and areas of development.

If you haven't identified or actively built a clear brand over the last several years, it is likely a little muddled and inconsistent across different audiences. Or maybe you've held several roles, and have not defined and strengthened the common thread. For example, your persona in the office may not be consistent with the content you post on social media or your role on the PTA. Maybe you began your career as an elementary school teacher, then moved to a customer service position. Those people who knew you as a teacher may have trouble seeing you in a business role, especially if you haven't redefined your new professional brand with former colleagues.

Whether you haven't paid much attention to your brand previously or perhaps there are a few behaviors that you've been meaning to change, the good news is you can start building the brand you want right now!

Don't Wave Your Red Flags

Responsibility—Reality—*Risk*—Resilience

A HIRER WILL ALWAYS be scanning a job seeker's experience for signs of potential danger and loss. You probably haven't had a seamless career journey. That doesn't mean you need to be branded a risk. Most professionals have a red flag or two. A red flag is not an automatic out, but rather a sign there's something worth digging into further. Maybe there's a gap in your resume because you cared for your ill mother or perhaps you had a few jobs that lasted less than one year. In a job search, just being a Switcher is a red flag. However, there are several other common red flags such as:

→ Employment gaps
→ Layoff or termination
→ Lack of a college degree
→ Job hopping
→ Being overqualified

It's easy to succumb to fear when you're feeling inferior. The key is to appear confident, not apologetic. Confidence breeds confidence—and confidence is something we all want as a part of our brand. So, don't wave your red flags and make these a part of your brand! There's no need to create *mental* obstacles for yourself to navigate. A career switch comes with its own *real* obstacles. Don't waste your energy on perceived ones.

To successfully get past red flags in the hiring process, don't dwell on what you're missing or the negatives. Rather, brand yourself in a positive way, give the hirer enough information to address the concern, and then move forward, discussing how you'll bring value to the organization and solve the department's pain points.

- **Take ownership.** If you were previously laid off, you might say, "When my company was acquired, several departments were consolidated due to an overlap in responsibilities. My position was impacted, so I took that opportunity to evaluate my strengths and am now looking to take my extensive experience in analytics to drive efficiencies in the recruiting process for a top firm like Acme." Spend precious interview time talking about the future and what you bring to the organization, rather than the past, which is behind you.

- **Remove emotion from the discussion.** While it's natural to feel uncomfortable or even defensive explaining tough situations, especially if they're still unhealed (like a recent layoff), showing that it bothers you will only lead the hirer to assume you're hiding something, even if you're not. Find a way to make peace with the situation before interviewing.

- **Watch your nonverbals.** Speaking rapidly, giving unnecessarily long explanations, avoiding eye contact, or fidgeting will betray you. Studies show people can tell when others are distorting, manufacturing, or withholding an emotion.[2] Interviews are inherently stressful. Don't give yourself more to worry about. Anticipate the tough questions, practice concise answers, and respond as if speaking about what you had for dinner last night: neutral and matter-of-fact.

- **Feel their pain.** As a Switcher, you'll face scrutiny. Even if you have a track record of success and can articulate how these experiences will be an asset, hirers will challenge you because you are not what they're accustomed to seeing and they want to avoid a loss. Be careful not to let your aggravation show. Appreciate that if the tables were turned, you would do your due diligence also. Acknowledge the concern, and approach it head-on with examples of where you have excelled with little training or limited direction. For example, "I can understand your hesitation about hiring a nontraditional candidate. Although I've not worked directly in this industry, I have a track record of excelling in ambiguous situations. One example is, a few months after accepting my last role, my immediate manager had to take an unexpected leave. Despite being new, I stepped up to run two of the largest accounts and ended up completing the deliverables without a hitch. I believe my ability to make strong connections and be resourceful enables me to step into new situations and find a way to create value."

If you're confident, other people will be confident *about* you. When you're at the interview table, remember you've earned your right to be there. Own it!

What's in Your Brand Bank?

Companies spend millions creating, defining, and communicating their brands, but individuals have only recently begun to realize the importance of professional branding. For example, Apple brilliantly markets their iPads, iPhones, and tablets, but if their products didn't deliver, they wouldn't remain popular for very long. Steve Jobs was a believer in the concept of a "brand bank," likening the building of a company's brand to deposits and withdrawals in a bank account. Positive interactions with customers contribute to the brand and negative interactions detract from it.[3]

You don't need to be perfect or constantly obsessing about your brand, but it should be top of mind so your behaviors are consistently aligned with the experience you want to deliver in your interactions. Although many professionals don't dedicate much attention or effort to building a brand, they really should. Fair or not, your brand drives more than you might realize in your career, including:

- What roles, promotions, or assignments you get
- What projects and teams you're asked to work on
- Who wants to associate with you
- Who is willing to go to bat for you
- Which clients you work with
- How much you earn, such as your bonus and raises
- What events and meetings you get invited to
- What information others share with you
- How easily you influence others

Steve Jobs's "brand deposit" analogy for Apple works the same for your individual brand. Whether or not you've paused to think about it, you have a professional reputation that's been building over time with deposits and withdrawals. You are already known for certain qualities, traits, and skills. Depending on how strong your current brand is and the level of change (industry, functional, or double Switcher) you're attempting to make, your network may have trouble seeing you in your new Plan A.

In fact, it's probably hardest for the people who know you *best* to see you in a new role, even though they support you and want you to succeed. Humans aren't comfortable with change (see Chapter Two), so friends and family might subconsciously torpedo your efforts by encouraging you to be the person you've always been. You've probably experienced this before, without even realizing it, when coworkers might be outwardly supportive of your diet, but continue to gently nudge you to eat the doughnuts they brought to the office. Your spouse might encourage you to train for the triathlon, but then coax you to snuggle in bed instead of going for an early jog.

When *you* change, the people around you experience the change as well. And if it's perceived as a positive change, they may feel some guilt they aren't doing it, too. It doesn't mean they don't support you; they may just have difficulty seeing you in a new way, especially the longer they've known you. So, you have some work to do!

Craft Your (New!) Brand in Five Steps

Your brand is a *guidepost,* acting as the foundation upon which your entire career strategy will be built. It is not your "elevator pitch," your resume summary statement, or even something that can be boiled down into words. Your brand is a *feeling* (remember how much weight others give to emotions in decision making) people have when reading your emails, viewing your social media, listening to your ideas in meetings, watching how you handle stress, observing who you associate with, and noticing how you present yourself. Over time, people weave all these observations together to identify your brand.

Your brand is how others come to know you and how they expect you to appear. That consistency is what builds trust over time. And that feeling of trust is central to any brand. When people read my online blog, they expect advice and tips related to enhancing their careers. It would be surprising or confusing if someone in my network went to my blog and found a random discussion about the business impact of healthcare marketing. This is not an area that has been associated with me.

But what if I'm a Switcher and healthcare marketing *is* my new focus? To get the attention of potential employers in this area, I need to start rebranding myself with my current network, since they will be integral in helping me achieve my new career goal. For Switchers, rebranding is essential. You want potential employers to visualize you as a fit for your chosen role and take a chance on you as a nontraditional candidate. This means you need a clear, consistent brand that aligns well with your target. And although it's true that brand is intangible and tricky to put into words, the best way to begin *rebranding* is by writing an initial brand statement.

If this is the first time you've thought about your brand, it may feel foreign or strange, so be patient and give it time to take shape. Also, keep in mind that a key part of having a strong brand is that you appeal to your intended audience, *but not to everyone.* This is important because, by definition, a solid brand will differentiate you from others who identify as doing similar work. One of my favorite marketing mantras is: If you appeal to everyone, you appeal to no one.

STEP 1. Know Your Goal and Your Audience's Pain Points

It's hard to build a brand if you don't have a specific goal and audience in mind, so you need to clearly answer the question, "What do I want to be known for and by whom?" For example, if you'd like to transfer to your company's office in Berlin, you may want to be known for your fluency in German. As a Switcher, your primary goal is made up of all the pieces in Plan A: your target role, company, geography, tasks, and so on. By this point, your Plan A should be clearly defined. Your audience will be the hiring decision makers and your network contacts, and you want to know a lot about them so you can show how your contributions will solve their pain points (see Chapter Three). Research each company you're targeting to learn about their strategic priorities, competition, and challenges. To add structure to your research, you may want to employ a mini-SWOT analysis (identify the audiences' **s**trengths, **w**eaknesses, **o**pportunities, and **t**hreats):

- What are the *strengths* of the industry, market, or company, and how are they being engaged?
- What is the main *weakness* of the industry, market, or company, and how can it be turned around?
- What changes or *opportunities* are happening now or predicted in the market or company (like regulations, technology, globalization)? Which of these are *threats*?
- Who are the key competitors and what differentiates them (*opportunities* and *threats*)?

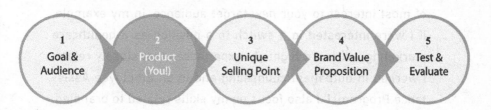

STEP 2. **Know the Product (You!)**

In a job search, *you* are the product you're selling. And presumably, you know yourself better than anyone. However, you may not have spent time reflecting on and mapping out your key experiences as thoroughly as you will in the next exercise, which will be a critical step in building your brand. It can be helpful to first lay out *all* your current and former roles, achievements, and personal characteristics to get a complete picture of everything that can be used to create your new brand. One effective way to do this is to build a "Who I Am" Map that details your past roles, accomplishments, skills, and values.

SWITCH ACTION

Build Your "Who I Am" Map

I'VE INCLUDED MY OWN "Who I Am" Map here as an illustration. To create yours in your journal, think deeply about every role you've held, including part-time, volunteer, summer jobs, and so on. Consider any credentials, awards, certifications, degrees, or other designations that you've earned, and any situations where you were asked to speak, be on an expert panel, lead a visible project, or figure out the solution to a challenging problem. Remember to include committees, special task forces, or achievements you're proud of. As you complete this exercise, have an open mind and include anything that comes into your head, whether or not it seems to align with your new career direction.

Once you've exhausted the columns, determine what will be of most interest to your *new* target audience. In my example, if I were interested in a switch to a position as a healthcare marketing writer, I'd highlight experiences that closely relate: I worked in outpatient counseling and in an Employee Assistance Program. I'd also focus on my skills related to branding, writing resumes, blogging, and social media. It doesn't necessarily matter *when* you held these roles, rather *what abilities* show how you fit the desired role. You won't be a perfect match because you aren't a traditional candidate. However, you likely have more experiences than you think that align with your new path. Dig deep!

KEY TITLES	KEY ACCOMPLISHMENTS	KEY EXPERTISE	PERSONALITY AND VALUES
• Licensed Psychologist	• Wrote/edited thousands of resumes; cover letters	• Panelist/Keynote at industry conference	• Dependable
• Recruiter/HRM	• Facilitated hundreds of seminars	• MS in Applied Behavioral Science	• Analytical
• National Radio Host	• Built a new global talent man-agement function and team	• Ph.D. in Psychology	• Driven
• Senior Consultant	• Managed largest client of firm ($14B earning $3M annually)	• Expat in Europe	• Productive
• Global Director	• Recognized as "One to Watch"	• Work with diverse global populations	• Organized
• Career Coach	• Exceeded Annual BD goals within six months of joining the firm	• SPHR certification	• Curious
• Certified Personal Trainer	• Implemented a firmwide career tool	• Extensive training in design and facilitation	• Creative
• Entrepreneur	• Published scientific research	• Hired and managed global/ virtual teams	• Open to Feedback
• Board Member	• Created a new Sirius XM show	• Deep assessment skills	• Planner
• Adjunct Professor	• Published a book	• Built and implemented global infrastructures and policies	• Introvert
• Victim Advocate		• Program and Project Management	• Likes a Challenge
• Operations Manager		• Career and Interview Coaching	• Health Conscious
• Market Researcher		• Deep industry expertise in talent/Human Resources	• Loves to Learn
• Outpatient Alcohol Counselor			• Independent
• Writer/Blogger			• Proactive
• Blackjack Dealer			
• Volunteer at Shelter			
• EAP Counselor			

STEP 3. **Know Your Differentiators**

Humans are complex, and our unique personalities form through a lifetime of diverse experiences. You have a *Unique Selling Point*, or USP, that sets you apart from others who do similar work. For example, Oprah Winfrey and Jerry Springer are both talk show hosts, but most would agree they have unique selling points that make their brands appeal to very different audiences.

Your USP is a critical part of your brand in a job search. No matter what your profession or background, something will set you apart from the competition in your field. Some examples might be that you:

- Are bilingual or multilingual
- Have a rare combination of industry skills (Lawyer and MBA)
- Possess an unusual outside accomplishment (you are an Olympian or Grammy winner)
- Have a special talent that is relevant (published author in your field, technically savvy)
- Completed an expat assignment or have extensive global or "in country" experience
- Bring an extensive network that broadens your ability to contribute
- Have a unique approach to your work or knack for something
- Possess unusually deep industry or product expertise

The list is endless. So figure out what makes you unique because your USP will help you answer the question, "*Why should we hire you over the other qualified candidates?"* A USP is your differentiator. It shows an employer how they will get even more value if they hire you. (A qualified applicant *plus* someone who can communicate in Portuguese with the Brazil office? Score!) Be very specific. If you simply introduce yourself as a talk show host, for example, it's up to others to fill in the gaps. Depending on their experiences, knowledge, and biases, they might conclude that you're like Jerry Springer when, really, you're more like Oprah. Don't give that power away! While you can't fully control how others experience you, you can influence it by what you communicate.

Your task as a Switcher is to *first* show a hirer you have the core skills to do the job, and *second* to use your differentiators as leverage to show your unique advantage. In Chapter Three I told Greg's story. He wanted to rebrand from a corporate attorney for a large pharmaceutical company to a product manager for wearable healthcare devices. Greg's USP includes first how he is a fit for the role and *then* how his additional skills add to his value. His USP might look something like this:

> Working in pharma for twelve years has given me a strong understanding of the healthcare landscape both domestically and abroad including an extensive network of vendors, customers, and executives in regulation and policy positions. My experience as an attorney has honed my expertise influencing win-win solutions without direct authority across business lines, which enables me to get things done efficiently.

It may take a little time to figure out your USP in relation to your intended industry, but keep working on it. Everyone has one (or more). Sometimes it's challenging to see yourself objectively in this way, so this may be a time to engage your friends to help (see the brand research exercise earlier in this chapter).

STEP 4. Identify Your Brand Value Proposition

Your Brand Value Proposition (BVP) describes how you solve your audience's pain points. Essentially, a BVP pulls together all the pieces we've discussed to create a *guidepost* for how you introduce yourself, what you choose to post online, the circles you need to network into, the projects you take on, how you show up, and much more. It will be the reason a hiring manager selects you. Here are some examples:

- Say you're an accountant in a global technology firm applying for recruiting roles in smaller tech companies with limited budgets. With your quantitative skills, you can analyze trends in the market to help forecast and manage hiring expenses more efficiently. In an interview you might say, "Having a deep appreciation for how technology firms function both financially and operationally, I'm able to identify the best talent while also focusing on cost-effective strategies to maximize the recruiting budget."

- Greg can utilize his extensive network of vendors to lower production costs on new products and can use his knowledge of global contracts and policy to cut through red tape that gets in the way of product distribution. With this BVP, he might say to his network, "After twelve years in pharma, I'm ready to expand my healthcare expertise and deepen my focus on technology as a product manager in the wearable devices industry. My related strengths include my ability to rally cross-functional teams around a core goal and cut through the red tape associated with doing business overseas due to my extensive vendor relationships and deep understanding of global policy."

While you will likely alter your specific words to meet your audience, mapping out your BVP is a critical step in your switch. Don't expect your contacts or the hiring manager to figure this out. *Do the work* so you can clearly show your value as it relates to your Plan A. Show them it's worth considering a Switcher, who may be risky initially, but can potentially offer greater value in the long run. Hiring is an investment. Show them you're worth investing in!

STEP 5. **Test and Evaluate**

A final, yet critical part of creating a successful brand is ensuring that others clearly understand your BVP. This is harder in some fields, particularly as roles become more complex. Here are some ways to ensure your brand is clear to others:

- Share your BVP with a few trusted colleagues and friends and ask if it resonates. What you say should still sound credible to them and be understandable, even if they don't know the field.
- Use an analogy for jobs that are more challenging to describe. For example, "I translate code for computers in the same way that a language interpreter converts French into English."
- Include a brief example that people can relate to, which deepens their understanding and helps your brand hit

home. Greg might talk about how he wants to manage the next FitBit for diabetes prevention instead of using terms like "wearable devices," which may not be clear to some.

Your first attempt at a BVP, especially for a career switch, will challenge you. Trust me, you have USPs and they're worth uncovering. And your target will definitely have pain points. So connect the dots and bring them together.

IN SUMMARY

Don't strive for perfect when crafting your brand because it will only lead you to wasted time and dead ends. Clarity comes through *action*, and change isn't linear. Those who find success have walked in many circles to get there, modifying as they go. Keep at it, and the ideas will come to you.

CHAPTER FIVE SWITCH POINTS

➜ You're always communicating your brand, consciously or not. You need to be intentional and cognizant of the messages you're relaying, so your audience starts to recognize a brand that aligns with your new career path.

➜ A key part of your brand is your USP (Unique Selling Point), which differentiates you from others with similar skills in a way that is of value for your audience.

➜ Your BVP (Brand Value Proposition) describes how you solve your audience's pain points. It's also your guidepost for how you choose to express your brand.

➜ Every candidate has potential red flags. The trick is not to dwell on these. Instead, focus on your strengths and the value you bring.

Your Career Story

Where Reason Meets Intuition

To decide on a candidate, hirers consider a combination of data (your skills and abilities) and intuition (their sense of your fit with the company). In Chapter Two, I talked about the role emotions play in decision making. To logically justify their decision before making an offer, hirers also want to understand the candidate's motivation—the *why*. This is the reason it sometimes takes so long to receive the offer: the hiring manager is still looking for the "why."

In this chapter, you'll discover how to make closing the deal easier for the hirer. As you work through the exercises, you will learn:

- Why the logic of your Career Story matters to hirers
- The three things hirers are evaluating when they look at potential candidates
- How to craft a killer response to "Why do you want this job?" that lands you an offer
- Strategies to persuade the company to take a chance on you
- Helpful tips to engage when the stress of the job search starts to wear on you

Logic Matters (A Lot)

When a company identifies a market need and decides to hire an employee, they will be evaluating three things in potential candidates.

- Their **ability** to perform the work (The "What")
- Their **fit** with the company or department (The "How")
- Their **motivation** to pursue this job (The "Why")

Hirers will weigh abilities, fit, and motivation differently depending on whether they're looking at a traditional candidate or a Switcher, as well as the type of switch the candidate is trying to make (industry, functional, or double switch). This is where *logic* (the "why" of your Career Story) matters—it can make the difference between getting an offer and getting passed over. Clarify your logic early on so you can share it with precision later.

Hired!

The "What" (Abilities)

Most job seekers focus on promoting their skills and related background to potential employers. Switchers worry that their lack of direct experience will be a deterrent. And it's true, it will be an obstacle. Hiring managers have a day job to perform. They want to bring in new team members painlessly, so many over-rely on current skill sets as a primary determining factor. (*"You've done this job before, so you'll hit the ground running and my life will be easier."*)

While you likely have transferable skills and abilities that apply across many functions and industries (e.g., strong negotiation skills), if a hiring manager is overly focused on your previous experience in traditional roles, it will be difficult for a Switcher to break into that department or company. You may be better off focusing your energy on companies that place a higher value on fit and motivation, where a hiring manager is more likely to recognize you as a valuable investment instead of a plug to fill a hole.

The "How" (Fit)

Luckily for Switchers, most managers realize skills can be developed, but traits like attitude and work ethic are stable, so they focus on finding a candidate who is also a good fit. They look at how a candidate's approach to tasks, personality characteristics, work habits, and communication style align with the current team or organizational culture. My client Natalie loved gadgets and online games, but had little direct technology experience in the workplace. She landed a help-desk role because of her outgoing nature and ability to communicate effectively with a variety of people. The hiring manager had the foresight to recognize this quality was lacking on the IT team, and was willing to spend a little more time training Natalie on the fuctional skills.

Switchers (especially industry Switchers) can capitalize on this fact, because organizational culture is unique to each company and emotion plays a role in all human decision making. Research has shown that hiring managers rate likability and positivity among their top traits, and these can often trump skills, especially in organizations that are known for being agile, diverse, and progressive. As one recent career advice article neatly summarizes, "If it comes down to two candidates, a hiring manager is more likely to choose the candidate with a positive attitude."[1]

A referral will go a long way here, since referred candidates are often a good "fit" for the company. This is one reason why so many companies have Employee Referral programs—a credible internal employee has usually already vetted the candidate's fit. Be likable, engage your network, and seek out cultures that are looking for characteristics you embody. Fit is impossible to fake for long, so finding a good match for yourself is equally important to *your* satisfaction.

The "Why" (Motivation)

Some hirers carelessly overlook motivation when they're considering traditional candidates, simply assuming they enjoy the work, know what they're getting into, and will automatically contribute to the team's success, which can lead to poor hiring decisions. Switchers face much deeper scrutiny into their motivation. When considering a Switcher, hirers are on alert so they'll wonder about your *reasons* for making a switch, asking: Why *this* role? Why *here* at our company? And why *now* at this point in your career? You'll need strong answers to these questions if you want to earn an offer.

This is where your Career Story comes in. Your Career Story is the answer to a common question: "What led you to apply to the open role at our company today?" (Or, to put it another way, "Why do you want this job?") Even if everything else has fallen into place for the hiring manager, this question is the "make it or break it" one that will tip the scales. Hirers need to know your switch isn't a whim. Your Career Story will also be critical when networking if you want to create ambassadors who advocate for you (more on that in Chapter Eight).

As a Switcher, your task is to convince the employer or your network that your career decision is well thought out, you've already demonstrated a commitment, the move fits into your grander career plan, and you understand your growth edges and have a plan for closing these gaps. A convincing Career Story should be:

- attention-getting
- compelling
- logical
- genuine

Here's an example of a Career Story that meets these four requirements:

After building my consulting expertise over the last four years working primarily with technology clients in consumer goods, I traveled to China on a long-term project to help one of our largest clients open a facility there. Although I spoke the language, I had little experience with policy and regulations that were critical to the success of the project. Through my contacts and research, I gained the knowledge to successfully complete the assignment, and realized that this type of work engaged my strengths, including negotiating with vendors, problem solving in the moment, and interpreting policy. Since PharmaTech, Inc. is in the process of expanding to Asia, I recognized a match between my background and your firm's goals and am interested in learning more.

SWITCH ACTION

Craft Your Career Story

TO BEGIN TO CRAFT the Career Story you'll use with your network and potential employers during your career switch, ask yourself these questions and answer them in your journal.

1. Why are you *really* making this change? Authenticity must be the basis of your answers. You don't need to (and shouldn't) share everything, but responses should be based on truth and rooted in logic.

2. What aspects of the story will resonate most strongly with your audience? Hirers are most concerned with your commitment to the new role or company, and the general process for how you came to the conclusion to pursue it. Avoid giving unnecessary details.

3. How can you make sense of your career history to show a hirer this move is a conscious, planned decision in your trajectory? What evidence do you have that you've already invested in and made progress toward this commitment? (Avoid phrases like "career change" or "transition" in your response. The goal is to show this is the next logical step.)

4. How have the above career steps prepared you for this role? Include transferable skills—boil them down to how they match the needs of the position you're applying to. If you're making a functional change but staying in the same industry, you may choose to highlight your deep industry expertise, for example.

5. Once you show how you're a match, next the hirer will want to know how you stand out from other candidates. What makes you different (USP)? How will this help you be effective in the

new role and company? Note: Keep this to a minimum in the early stages of the discussion unless probed.

6. Lastly, your story might include how this new role supports your future goals. Don't position it as a stepping stone if you see it that way; rather, show you're making conscious choices and how the contributions you make in *this* role support your long-term career strategy. Keep this brief.

Credibility Builders

If you're asked deeper questions on your Career Story, have specific examples and accomplishments to back up your statements:

1. What value has your past work created? Describe major accomplishments and unique contributions you've made to your present and past organizations.

2. How do these accomplishments and skills contribute to your success in this next role? Choose experiences most relevant to your target.

Taking time to flesh out your Career Story will make every future conversation in your job search process—networking, interview, salary negotiations—*much* easier. You'll already have answers to the tough questions and will gain greater clarity on your Plan A and BVP in the process. Remember, the process is iterative, so appreciate that you'll continue to acquire insights and make tweaks.

You are asking the employer to take a chance on you, so the more you can anticipate and assuage a hirer's concerns, the more likely you will be to get the offer.

What to Do When You Start Hating the Job Search

Responsibility—Reality—Risk—Resilience

ANXIETY. REJECTION. FRUSTRATION. JUDGMENT. Ambiguity. Unfairness. It's easy to understand why people dislike the job search, especially Switchers. Although most people are excited by the prospect of *landing* a new job, the actual job search *process* isn't an inherently enjoyable experience. In fact, it kind of sucks. If you think about it, though, looking for a job is not so different from, say, purchasing a new car. It's exciting to visualize yourself in a shiny hybrid, but most people dread the buying process—dealing with aggressive sales associates, haggling over price, selecting coverage terms.

Many of the most exciting things in life require a lead-up process that is anything but comfortable or easy. And sometimes the advice to "enjoy the journey" just doesn't cut it. If you really want something, though, don't let common barriers stop you from attaining your goal. For most people, the sweet taste of success is worth dealing with the temporary discomfort. When you're feeling discouraged, here are some ideas to get you through the hurdles:

- **Plan for the 30 percent.** Even the best planners experience situations they can't control or foresee. When preparing for a major change, incorporate enough cushion into the planning to allow for 30 percent of your plans to go wrong. For example, in the job search, leave 60 minutes to get to the interview rather than 40 minutes. This will significantly decrease added stress in an already stressful process.

- **Take a tip from Tom Hanks.** In the movie *A League of Their Own*, when Tom's best player quits the baseball team right before the playoffs because things got too hard, Tom comes back with one of the best lines in the movie: "It's the hard that makes it great."[2] Successful professionals overcome incredible difficulties to get to the gold. Go the extra mile.

- **Focus on the benefits.** Building on the last point, remember that the people who are most agile, adaptable, and resilient are also those who have conquered many challenges. With each new setback you crush, you'll be able to handle future struggles with more ease. You'll be comfortable taking greater risks, which will lead to even more success!

Nothing worth having comes easy. But that's okay—you've got this!

Convince People to Roll the Dice on You

All too often, the most qualified person doesn't get the job, the person with the best connections does. But you know what? This is excellent news for Switchers who can market themselves effectively! As we talked about in Chapter Two, hiring mistakes are costly, and companies err on the side of hiring traditional candidates who seem safer, rather than career changers. To combat this, you need a solid strategy. Once you have a clear Plan A, BVP, and Career Story, there are a few more things you can do to reassure the hirer you're *worth* rolling the dice on.

Close Your Knowledge Gaps

Experience is experience, whether you receive a paycheck or not. Take on an internal project. Create your own part-time gig in the field you're pursuing. How? You need to be resourceful! Srini was interested in making a switch to finance from a supply chain role. I suggested he volunteer his time in another area of his company to learn how corporate investments worked. He had to add five hours a week to his already busy schedule, and had to get his boss's buy-in, but he ultimately ended up hitting it off with the finance team who were impressed with his initiative. If, like Srini, you volunteer your time, you'll find that, in addition to building skills, you'll expand your network and have a chance to test the waters on your career switch before fully making the leap. (Spoiler alert: Srini decided finance wasn't the path for him after all—and his volunteer experience helped him figure this out before he'd invested a lot of time and effort.)

Clarity comes through action! While gaining experience on your own time may feel like a big commitment, if you're not willing to do it, you should question how motivated you are to make the switch right now. After all, if *you* don't invest, why should a company?

Speak Their Language

If you're coming from another industry—for example making a switch from the military to a corporate role—use language that connects you to the interviewer or industry professionals, rather than distances you. Instead of talking about your "platoon," use the word "team." If you have a background in education and are switching to business, use words like "agenda" or "strategic goals" instead of "lesson plan." Your aim in the interview is to build a positive relationship with your potential boss, so this subtle change in verbiage can make a difference in convincing her to see you as a "fit" for the company. Once again—do the work *for* the hirers rather than expecting *them* to figure out how to translate your skills into solutions for their pain points.

Communicate a Consistent Brand

It can feel disappointing to remove qualifications or achievements from your social media platforms or resume when you've worked hard to earn these credentials. But you're bound to have some accomplishments that don't align with your new career path and will muddy your brand when a recruiter looks at your background (see Chapter Five for more on rebranding). Many skills are transferable, so a simple rewording may do the trick for some projects. However, you might need to remove other achievements entirely to be taken seriously as a candidate. Trang was transitioning from academia to the corporate sector. She started getting bites only *after* she removed her Ph.D. credential from her profile. Seek objective feedback to ensure you're marketing yourself *clearly* to your new audience. While these credentials may help you differentiate yourself at a later stage in the hiring process (as your USP, for example), initially they may knock you out of the running due to preconceived biases and stereotypes.

Put Their Minds at Ease

If interviewers ask about your nontraditional background, acknowledge their concern and show how you'll overcome it. One way to do this is to share experiences from your past when you were new to situations and achieved success. For example,

> When starting my last job, the only person who really knew the company inventory database had already left. Although I'd never used this system, I was able to contact the company who created the software and get up and running within one week. My new boss appreciated this since the busy holiday season was fast approaching and the store would have difficulty managing inventory without the daily reports I was tasked with creating.

Past success is one indicator of future success, so examples like this can go far in demonstrating your ability to apply your transferable skills and adapt to novel situations quickly.

Be Confident (Not Apologetic)

Focus on the value you *bring* to the job rather than the experience you don't have (yet!). No one has every qualification, even traditional candidates. Sincere motivation, diligent preparation, and a track record of success—even in a completely different role—can be powerful. I hired a nontraditional candidate over a well-qualified, traditional one strictly on this principle, despite concern from my team. Shannon's references were stellar, she had a history of consistent achievement in previous roles, and she was deeply curious during the hiring process. While I think the other candidate would have done fine, Shannon's Career Story convinced me that she was a better choice for the long term, which is important to a hirer who doesn't want to go through the hiring process again anytime soon. Confidence breeds confidence, and skills can be learned.

Engage the "Likability" Effect

A friend of mine interviewed for a position and the hiring manager talked about himself, his family, and his goals for the *entire* interview. My friend listened attentively until the end of the interview, when the hirer asked him if he knew how to use Excel (to which he confidently responded "yes"), and he got the job on the spot! While this wasn't the best hiring strategy on the company's side, there are multiple studies that show likability, defined by factors such as warmth and trustworthiness, surpassed competence when individuals were making decisions to hire, promote, or invest money in others.[3] This makes sense when we realize we spend nearly half of our waking hours at work.

According to former Harvard Business School professor Amy Cuddy, 80 to 90 percent of a first impression is based on likability and competence, but here's the kicker: In order for competence to even matter, people must trust you *first*.[4] This is the *opposite* of what most people do when networking. Most are taught to begin with a "thirty-second pitch" that highlights skills, but which according to Cuddy's research, likely *distances* you from the person you're trying to impress. Yes, competence is important, but the *order* of relaying it in new relationships matters. Build trust *first* by asking questions, being engaged, and demonstrating positive body language (such as by eye contact and smiling).

Neuroscientist Diana Tamir found the brain gets more pleasure when you're *talking about yourself* than it does from food or money![5] Use this to your advantage by simply allowing others to speak about themselves. This strategy (and decent Excel knowledge) is what got my friend hired!

Match First, Stand Out Second

A USP (Unique Selling Point) adds to your candidacy and makes you stand out. But bringing it up too early in the process may get you weeded out. Let's get into the mind of the hirer. Before they care about your USP, they want to *first* know you can do the job. They must believe you have the foundational qualifications to be successful in the role; only then do they want to know what sets you apart from the competition. Match the qualifications of the job as closely as possible *first,* then discuss additional relevant abilities you can contribute. Your USP is critical, and timing is key (see Chapter Five for more on USP).

Put Their Needs First

Successful Switchers communicate their abilities and interests in ways that demonstrate how they will *benefit the company*. The hirer isn't interested in what *you* want or what you're interested in learning. They care about hiring someone who is motivated and capable of performing effective work with little hand-holding. In the interview, in your cover letter, and on social media, ensure the expertise you share clearly points out how the company will benefit. Take a look at the following example:

☞ **Before:** "I'm a project manager with ten years of global experience in healthcare managing multiple projects. In addition, I've earned an MBA with a specialty in strategy, and speak fluent Hindi. I'm interested in a role that allows me to use the strategic planning skills I've gained, while expanding my international exposure."

☞ **After:** "My particular expertise in project management is mobilizing diverse teams across cultures to effectively execute on a common goal. In addition, my knowledge of strategic planning enables me to see multiple contingencies when unexpected challenges arise. Your company's operations span three continents, and I'm confident my ten years of global experience, deep business acumen from my MBA, and proven collaboration skills will enable me to hit the ground running to ensure a seamless transition in this role."

Notice the difference? The first version was mostly a list of skills, degrees, and interests, which means the hiring manager is left doing the work to figure out how it will solve her problems. The second version conveys similar skills and interests, but in an *applicable* way, so the hiring manager can clearly see a connection to the position. The *before* was impressive, but the *after* will land the job!

IN SUMMARY

You already know you can be successful in this career change. Now you need to convince the hiring manager. Much of that comes down to psychology: recognizing the subtleties of fear, bias, loss, and emotion in the decision making process. It depends on communicating your value to show how you'll achieve results for the company. Practice your messages and recognize the power that your words can have—either in your favor or against. Your Career Story isn't just an afterthought; it's the information that will seal the deal.

CHAPTER SIX SWITCH POINTS

→ Hirers care about three things: abilities, fit, and motivation. While each has its place, Switchers can have the most advantage over traditional candidates on the latter two.

→ Your Career Story is what will convince the hiring manager to pull the trigger and make the offer. It should be attention-getting, compelling, logical, and genuine.

→ How you communicate, including the words you choose and the timing of the information, will make a difference to convince the hirer to take a risk. Practice your messages to ensure you connect with the interviewer.

→ Keep perspective. The job search is an inherently tough process, but that's what makes landing your switch so awesome!

What Got You Here Won't Get You There

The Proactive Job Search

As with most things in life, there isn't a one-size-fits-all process for a successful job search. While it's comforting to believe there is a cause-effect relationship or linear set of steps (send resume → get interview → receive offer), this *reactive* approach to finding a job doesn't yield great results, especially for Switchers. One primary problem is that, by most estimates, about 80 percent of available jobs are *never posted publicly*, especially mid-level to senior-level roles. If a company plans to fire their CFO at the end of the quarter, you can be certain they are *not* posting that role online. Most employers prefer avoiding a public search: A CareerBuilder survey found that *before posting a job, 72 percent of employers first look at internal resources including referrals, their own resume database, the talent community, and their network.*[1] This means that if you're only applying for jobs you find online—that is, engaging in a *reactive* job search—you're competing with 100 percent of the applicants for fewer than possibly a quarter of the available jobs. You don't need to be a math whiz to realize those aren't great odds.

In this chapter, you will learn:

- How vital networking is for a Switcher
- Why the online job search and working with a headhunter is a waste of a Switcher's energy and what to do instead
- How to craft a results-based resume no matter what your profession
- A quick technique to make writing great cover letters easy
- How to use social media to promote your new brand
- How to feel empowered by changing one word

Nontraditional Candidate? You Need a Nontraditional Job-Search Process

The Einstellung Effect is a psychological principle that describes what happens when our preconceived notions blind us to a better way of doing something. This cognitive trap tricks us into resorting to what has worked *before*, rather than finding the best solution to the current problem. For example, when seasoned medical doctors make mistakes, it's usually due to the Einstellung Effect—the experience of a prior patient with similar symptoms may lead a doctor to prescribe the same treatment to a new patient, even if it isn't the optimal solution. The biological tendency of the brain to simplify processes creates a barrier to seeing the ideal course of action, and in some cases, leads to completely missing what's actually going on. So, what you already know may in fact hurt you.

When the internet job search was born, it became the go-to method of finding new employment. Now, when the notion of a career change arises, most job seekers begin their search online. But the internet has become saturated, and what used to be an effective process is now generally a useless time-suck. Many job seekers are seduced by this reactive process, because applying to posts on big job sites offers more structure and seemingly less ambiguity. It also requires the least effort, but little effort leads to little reward. People may feel productive emailing resume after resume to open jobs on the clearinghouse sites, but be careful not to get caught in a cognitive trap. Switchers can't have the luxury of illusion. There are several reasons why applying online often leads to zero opportunities:

☞ **The jobs are often picked over.** Think about how you hire when you have an open position. Is your first step to pay large sums of money to post the role on big job sites? Probably not. First, you likely think about people you have worked with previously. Many jobs are filled by managers bringing in their former team members. Then, you inquire with your network. Is there anyone your trusted contacts might recommend for the role? Guess what? The companies *you're* applying to are taking this approach, too. If networking fails to produce a candidate, they'll next post the position internally, so only current employees in the organization have access to it (although you can, too, if you have a network contact inside the company!). If there are still no bites, the role will be posted on the company's public website (which is free and tends to attract applicants who have a direct interest in the organization), and then finally on the mega-job sites. So, how many of the most interesting, highest-paid, sought-after roles do you think make it to the mega-job sites? Awesome jobs are usually filled before the previous employee's chair is cold, so they're rarely advertised.

☞ **A robot is making the decisions.** Applicant Tracking Systems (ATSs) are recruiting software that weed out applicant resumes based on keywords and other preprogrammed data. They are the Switcher's nemesis! Since ATSs were implemented, only 25 percent of all resumes submitted online get viewed by human eyes.[2] Unless you're a very close match for the job on paper, have perfect timing, and use appropriate formatting, you'll end up stuck in resume cyberspace, while blissfully dreaming about the job you'll never get.

☞ **The job is already spoken for.** In some companies, it's policy to post all jobs publicly and interview external candidates, even if they've already identified a qualified referral or internal candidate. Unless the internal candidate turns down the role, your chances of getting this job are slim.

☞ **The job has expired.** When was the last time you cleaned out the condiments in your refrigerator? Companies are no different. It's not unusual for them to leave a job posted online long after it's been filled and the new employee is happily receiving a paycheck. Many online job postings are like that expired jar of mayonnaise in the back of your fridge.

☞ **It's the perfect job.** Have you ever come across a job that seemed ridiculously ideal? Unfortunately, it's tricky to regulate what is posted online and scammers are more than happy to prey on eager job seekers. Trust your gut: If it seems too good to be true, it usually is.

☞ **Everyone's applying.** Jobs posted online receive an average of 200 applicants, with top companies receiving even more. (Google once received 70,000 resumes in one week!)[3] Even if half these applicants are not qualified, that is some stiff competition!

So, should job seekers just cancel their Wi-Fi? Not exactly. Job boards, social media, and company websites are useful for research and enhancing your network. About 20 percent of job seekers *are* finding some success in online searches, particularly for jobs that pay less than $60,000. But this percentage is mostly for near-perfect matches, and not Switchers.

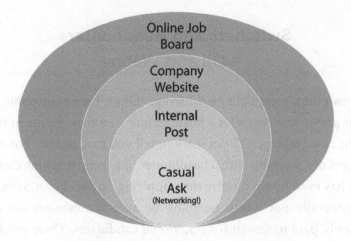

The Stages of Sourcing for a Job Opening

So don't get caught in an illusion just because it feels good. You need to create your own structure. In a *proactive* job hunt, actively identify companies you'd like to work for based on your Plan A and engage your network to get a foot in the door. This is an effective strategy that I'll walk through in Chapter Eight. According to research, referrals are the number one source of hiring volume and quality for employers. Some surveys show that fewer than 7 percent of total *applicants* come from the referral pool, which are much better odds for a Switcher.[4]

Once you have a clear Plan A and solid Brand Value Proposition (BVP), make networking the *first* step in your process and submitting your resume the *second* step. This gets you past the inherent bias, robots, and misinformation, to network *directly* into an interview. It's usually the *only* path to a career change. If you feel apprehensive about this, you're not alone. Networking *is* harder than sitting behind a laptop clicking "Send," but it's also infinitely more effective. Because so few people rely on it as their primary technique, there's a lot less competition. Don't worry, we'll address the process of building and engaging a network in detail in Chapters Eight and Nine. You're probably much better at it than you think!

Switchers and Headhunters
= Oil and Water

At this point, you might be thinking, "Okay, I see your point. But what about working with a headhunter? Can they get me in front of the best employers?" I'm sorry to tell you this, but no. For most job seekers, working with a headhunter or executive search consultant has even lower returns than applying online. For a Switcher, it's generally not worth pursuing because headhunters are customarily paid to search for *traditional* candidates. There are a lot of myths and assumptions about what headhunters actually do, so before you start down this path and get disappointed, here's a quick overview to consider:

☞ Headhunters filled fewer than 6 percent of the total open jobs in 2013 and only 3 percent the year before.[5] *HR Examiner* put the odds at "about 1 in 28,520 (.0035 percent) that your conversation with a headhunter will land you a job."[6] Headhunters typically are only helpful if you're looking for a very senior-level (C-Suite) role or a specialized, difficult-to-fill position.

☞ Headhunters are paid by the company (contingent search consultants earn, on average, 30 percent of a hire's base pay), which means their priority is finding what the organization wants, not what the job seeker wants. They won't be motivated to "sell" a nontraditional candidate to their well-paying customer, who is looking for a specific skill set. If you don't have 10–15 years in the industry and function they're looking for, which as a Switcher you don't, a headhunter won't be interested.

☞ With networking websites like LinkedIn, headhunters have powerful search tools and are easily able to find candidates they want. They build their pipeline with executives who have a history of the skills their clients request. If your social media is aligned with what headhunters are looking for, they will no doubt find *you* (see Chapter Thirteen for more on how to get recruiters knocking on your door).

Headhunters are sales experts, not career coaches. They don't have the time or the expertise to help you figure out what you should or could do. This isn't something you should delegate to a third party anyhow. Your career is a big deal and while getting advice and insight can be helpful, no one can tell you what the right path is.

A favorite article on this topic is titled "Headhunters Find People, not Jobs," by Nick Corcodilos of Ask The Headhunter fame. From over thirty years of experience, Nick makes it abundantly clear: "*Headhunters don't find jobs for people. If you are a good potential candidate for a specific job, the headhunter's job is to find you.*"[7]

Still apprehensive about networking? Remember, some companies (especially smaller ones like startups) rely heavily on employee referrals to fill positions, so a proactive search may be the *only* way to gain access to job openings. Also, many companies reward their employees for bringing in new talent, so you may be helping your contacts earn a nice referral bonus by asking them to pass your resume along.

With these perspectives on applying online and headhunters, adjust your expectations and time accordingly. If you have twelve hours each week for your search, spend at least nine of them talking to your connections and networking, then use the rest for mission-critical research, evaluating your strategy, practicing your messages, and building your new brand.

Life Is a "Choose To"

Responsibility—Reality—Risk—Resilience

IF YOU PAY CLOSE attention, you'll notice yourself frequently saying things like, "I wish I could help, but *I have* to take the kids to soccer," "*I need* to stay in this crappy job for the paycheck," or "I wanted to go to the gym, but *had to* work late." In life, there are very few "have to's" (or the closely related "need to"). While something may *feel* like a "have to" because you don't like the consequences of *not* doing it, most things in life are actually a "choose to."

For example, you could pursue a job you love, but which may pay less. But, you are *choosing* not to make the sacrifice. No one is forcing you to do anything. We choose to spend our time exactly how we want. Hearing this can be frustrating and initial responses are usually defensive. But when we think about it, we have a lot of freedom to choose our actions. We choose to hit snooze instead of get up to jog. We choose to apply online, rather than reach out to new contacts. We choose to stay at the office and skip dinner with the family. None of these is a "have to," although you might convince yourself it is. ("If I don't stay late, my boss will fire me!") The hard truth might be you're avoiding a difficult conversation with your boss, or possibly have a reason for choosing to work late that you don't care to admit. Change is hard, and the devil you know can be seductive.

The more "have to's" we create in life, the more stuck and demotivated we feel. When something is framed as a "have to," it sucks the joy out of it ("I have to cook dinner for the family"). When something is framed as a choice, it feels empowering (e.g., "I can't wait to try that new ratatouille recipe"). This simple shift in perspective and word choice gives you an instant boost in energy.

In a career switch, "have to's" can be a tempting rationalization to remain stuck. "I have to wait until . . .", "I need to be sure of . . .", and so on. Are these statements true, or are they a way of evading an unknown situation? Using the term "choose to" psychologically makes you feel more in control of the situation versus being a victim of circumstance. When you feel in control, you're able to see new options ("I choose to stay late to finish the report, and instead will go to the gym tomorrow morning").

We're adding unnecessary stress to our lives by framing everything as a "have to." Why not start tomorrow by saying, "I choose to wake up early, hit the gym, and have a productive day at work"? The difference you feel may surprise you.

The Six-Second Resume

Despite the threats (or promises) that innovations like social media and infographics will replace resumes, this hasn't happened yet. Most companies still require applicants, including referred candidates, to submit a standard resume when applying for a position. So, for now, resumes are a necessary tool in your job switch. Take the time to do it right. While there are many useful resources available to help you craft a great resume, here is some advice with Switchers' needs in mind.

With a foot in the door through a referral, your resume will be sure to follow. It's great to get your resume looked at by a hirer, but don't get too excited just yet. You might be surprised (and maybe a little irritated) to learn that the average hiring manager will spend a mere six seconds reviewing your resume. So, you'll want to make it stellar. Out of those six seconds, recruiters spend four seconds looking at four areas:

- Your job titles
- The companies where you worked
- Your job start and end dates
- Your education[8]

They'll likely spend the remaining two seconds glancing at your profile section at the top (and yes, you must have one as a Switcher!) or other accomplishments that leap off the page to catch their eye. With so little time to capture attention, and the inherent challenge of conveying so much on a piece of paper, you need to differentiate yourself. Be sure to connect with your audience through the language they use instead of distancing yourself from them with jargon or irrelevant information from your old industry or function. While a resume will rarely be your entrée into a new job as a Switcher, even if you get a referral, you still need an effective one to pass along. Follow these suggestions to craft a resume that will grab attention.

Create a Strong Profile

A powerful profile or summary statement at the top of your resume can influence what the reader concludes about you. A reader's eye will focus on the top third of the page, so use this section to share your relevant experience, skills, and accomplishments. Since you're a Switcher, your most relevant experience might be a few years old or even volunteer work, so the summary is your best friend. Use it to draw attention to your most *applicable* experience, however far in the past. The key points highlighted up top will become the lens through which hirers will view the rest of the resume. Focus on how your skills and experience can solve the organization's problems, *not* what you are seeking. Put their needs first. Skip the obsolete "Objective" section in favor of a targeted, results-laden profile that shows what value *you* bring. Recall Greg from Chapter Three. See his profile statement, next page.

Although Greg is currently an attorney who spends much of his time on contracts, he doesn't use this language. Instead, he targets the *relevant* skills he gained as a corporate lawyer in a pharma company—his global experience, leadership abilities, extensive contacts, tech savvy, and negotiating skills—and demonstrates how

HEALTHCARE | TECHNOLOGY | CUSTOMER RELATIONS

Agile Influencer with 12+ years' experience successfully navigating the healthcare landscape both *domestically and abroad* through building an extensive network of vendors, customers, and executives in regulation and policy positions to cut through red tape and *surpass goals by up to 20%*. Demonstrated expertise *negotiating win-win solutions in deals averaging $1.5–$2M* without direct authority across business lines and country borders to drive progress. Adept at engaging technology solutions to *simplify processes and expand possibilities*, and passionate about rallying teams around strategic initiatives that positively impact healthcare advancement.

he can put them to work as an attractive candidate for a product management position. (If you need a refresher on how to do this, flip back to Chapter Three.)

Skip the Job Description

Your resume should read less like a job description and more like the introduction for your lifetime achievement award. Accomplishments and results get noticed and have impact; a list of tasks or passive responsibilities won't. Don't believe me? Look at these two very different ways of summarizing your career experience:

☞ **Summary 1:** Head Sales Manager for the Northeast and Mid-Atlantic Regions, including multiple territories and 13 Sales Reps.

☞ **Summary 2:** Drove up annual sales by 23% across 7 territories in the Northeast and Mid-Atlantic Regions by motivating a team of 13 Sales Reps to exceed quarterly goals in 9 of the last

10 sales cycles, bringing in $7.5M in revenue over the last 3 years, with over $2.5M in new business.

Both statements include numbers and specifics, but which would convince you to take a second look at this candidate and want to learn more? Depending on your role, you might not be able to quantify your achievements with precise data. But it's still essential that you translate for your audience *how the work you did benefited* your company. It's up to you to let hiring managers know the value of your work in terms of the success it brought the company.

For corporate jobs, effective results can be broadly boiled down to 1) making money or 2) saving money. *How* you accomplish these goals varies depending on your role, but it might include increasing efficiency or decreasing waste, reducing risk or increasing profit margins, increasing client satisfaction or reducing employee turnover. The more relevant details you can offer (actual numbers, scope, and other specifics), the more credible and impressive the accomplishment. For example:

☞ Increased online product page views by 40%, which led to a year-over-year gain in sales of 19%, by designing a user-friendly web interface for global customers.

If your current or previous roles aren't directly numbers-driven, here's a simple trick to help you think about how the work you do positively impacts the company. Ask yourself: "What would happen if I *didn't* do my job?" For example, if you're an administrative assistant, what would happen if you didn't keep the calendar organized, proofread the reports, and coordinate the travel? Well, it's likely that your executive team wouldn't be nearly as effective in their roles and the profits of the company would suffer. So, one bullet on your resume might read:

☞ Ensured stakeholder deliverables were met and company operations ran smoothly by organizing and coordinating the global travel schedules for four busy C-Suite Executives contributing to $150MM in new business this past year.

Yes, it may be an indirect result of your role, but let's face it: If your position was not critical to keeping the company afloat, you wouldn't be receiving a paycheck. So *now* is the time to learn how your daily tasks impact the bottom line. Ask around and delve into public company reports to uncover your department's budget, quarterly gains, customer feedback scores, and data to understand the impact of your role. It's all a ripple effect, and you are likely contributing more than you think. When you're effective at your job, it can be difficult to see everyday tasks as accomplishments. Maybe you're an office manager for a regional retail business. What would happen if you didn't maintain the inventory, track expenses, and ensure all the shifts were covered? Chaos would ensue and it wouldn't be long before the business was in jeopardy. So how about:

☞ Maintained a sufficient supply of $750K in inventory for a seasonal business with three warehouses across the Northwest region to meet the demands of our more than 30,000 customers while remaining competitively priced.

When you're effective at your job, it can be difficult to see everyday tasks as accomplishments. However, when you imagine what could go wrong if no one was there to do your job, suddenly it's easy to see the value you bring to the company every day.

Take a critical look at your experience and focus on the accomplishments that most closely align with your Plan A to ensure your brand is clear. You may need to remove some achievements that you are proud of (which is difficult!), but it's better than the risk of steering the reader in the wrong direction—or worse, *no* direction.

Use an Effective Layout

Studies using heat sensors have shown that people tend to read re-sumes in an "F" pattern: across the top (your Summary), down the left margin (your companies, titles, and strong action verbs), and across the top middle (usually your most recent job).[9] Be strategic about where you place things so they stand out to the reader. Stick to a reverse-chronological resume (most recent job, followed by the prior job), and avoid using a functional-style resume (grouping your experience into categories based on competence areas rather than by job or company). Although functional resumes were once recommended for career changers, newer research shows recruiters prefer a traditional reverse chronological resume and view a func-tional resume as an instant red flag that a job seeker is attempting to hide something like a gap in employment, career switch, or job hopping.[10]

Show, Don't Tell

Scan your resume for empty phrases that aren't backed by specific accomplishments (that is, fluff). Don't write you are a great team player; give an example that has an emotional impact on the reader and leaves an impression: "Partnered with the client team at the eleventh hour to help complete a significant deliverable for our largest client, enabling the region to exceed Q2 earnings."

Another way to show your value is to highlight times when you were recognized by someone else, like a superior or a client, for work well done. Consider using verbs like "Awarded," "Selected," "Recognized," "Recruited," or "Promoted" to kick off a few of the bullet points on your resume. Any examples of situations or projects where you had to learn quickly are also beneficial for Switchers, because they show you are adaptable and are successful in new situations.

Instead of lifeless phrasing like "*Worked with the accounting team ...*" use dynamic verbs that offer a powerful image ("*Collaborated with . . .*"). These words have more impact on the page. If you use "*Responsible for . . .*" on your resume, be aware that this passive phrase is almost always followed by a job description, not an accomplishment. Fix it. Use "Managed," "Led," "Initiated," or "Directed" instead. Get creative—think about verbs you can easily act out in charades, like *built, streamlined, transformed, drove, juggled, revamped, designed.*

Finally, avoid overused and meaningless clichés such as "results-oriented," "excellent communication skills," or "analytical thinker," which don't differentiate you. You have limited space on a resume, so only include words that reflect the unique value you bring.

Make It Inviting

Avoid using paragraphs or bullet points more than three lines long. The more white space on the document, the more inviting it will be. Don't squish things with eight-point type and nonexistent margins. If your resume is written with impact, focused, and aligned with your Plan A, you don't need to list everything you've done in your career. A few well-positioned achievements speak volumes. Consider carefully whether to include experience older than fifteen to twenty years, which may unfortunately open you to age bias or clutter the resume with irrelevant or obsolete information. If your pertinent experience is from early in your career, use your profile to highlight it. You never want the *great* stuff to get lost in the good stuff!

Speak Their Language

To learn to speak their language, you *should* get online and review job descriptions in your target field, especially if you're changing industries or functions. Research current industry lingo and ensure you're using the latest business terminology for what you're targeting. Adopting language familiar to the reader helps establish a connection and demonstrates that you understand their playing field. If your internal job title is "Evangelist II" at your company, it's fine to put that in parentheses and identify yourself as a sales manager, which more accurately reflects your role and responsibilities in the larger market. Honesty is important, but so is clarity!

Be Proud!

Your resume is a marketing document. It needs to entice the reader. This is not a place to be humble, because the guy behind you won't be! Include relevant achievements, awards, honors, and other accomplishments that demonstrate your value. In my experience, more job seekers err on the side of being too modest, and what seems like bragging is music to a hiring manager's ears. It's not *what* you say, but *how* you say it that makes something boastful, so engage a friend for candid feedback.

Yes, you must be truthful; you won't get past the interview if you can't speak intelligently about what is on your resume. However, delve deeply. Tasks or projects that felt routine to you very well may impress others. Look at past performance reviews for ideas or get input from a former boss or colleague.

The Dreaded Cover Letter Made Easy

Every time you send out your resume—whether you networked into a company or applied online—include a cover letter that is customized and well written. It demonstrates interest and shows you're willing to go the extra mile, and for Switchers this is your chance to highlight specifically how you will solve the company's pain points. Don't overemphasize the fact that you're making a change, but do point out steps you've already taken to become successful in this new profession. Hirers will likely read your cover letter *after* your resume (if at all), but don't lose an opportunity by short-changing this step. A few key tricks will make the process effective and relatively painless. Create a cover letter shell that can be tailored, versus re-created, for each job application. Once you have the basic shell, since you have a focused Plan A, you'll just need to switch out specifics like company name, title of the role, and key strengths. You can create a solid cover letter using four *brief* paragraphs:

1. **Opening Paragraph.** Grab the reader's attention with the first sentence through an industry statistic, quote, or the name of the person who referred you. Avoid the overused and boring, *"Please find enclosed my resume . . .".* Connect with the reader and show how you can solve the company's problems.

2. **Second Paragraph.** Identify three to four strengths that align with the needs of the job. Show how you'll use these skills to make an impact. Consider bullet points to add some white space and break up the paragraph format. This also draws the reader's eyes to the meat of the letter.

3. **Third Paragraph.** Include additional reasons why you're a fit for the company and the role. Reiterate your motivation for and dedication to this specific career path.

4. **Closing Paragraph.** End strong. Thank the reader and let them know you will follow up. A call-to-action is bold (not blah!).

This sample cover letter was written from the perspective of a customer service manager looking to make the functional switch to business development.

Dear Ms. Myers,

Lily Israel spoke very highly of the Sales Team at Kerapac Telecom and the culture of putting the customer first. Cultivating relationships to deliver exceptional results is what I do best. Whether in a startup or global organization, I have consistently increased client satisfaction through my ability to develop trust and deliver quality. Further, being in customer service for both telecom and media has given me a deep understanding of customers' expectations and concerns, which puts me in a better position to sell them products that meet their varied needs.

When looking to hire a Business Development Manager, it's critical to find someone who can bring in new customers and represent the reputation of the organization. Some highlights of my career that align with these core requirements include:

- As a customer service lead at Novohart Mobile, I received the highest number of new referral cases from previous customers I had assisted, generating over $64k in new leads. In addition, I was asked to be the primary agent for our largest client due to my ability to diffuse tough situations and find creative win-win solutions.

- At Gravitasity Media, I was selected to onboard staff members due to my ability to effectively explain our complex products and services packages. During my time, I trained 22 new team members; more than half are now in supervisory roles with the company.

Delivering value to clients has been the focus of my 11-year career, and as my resume highlights, I've consistently excelled at quickly learning new processes and services, building lasting relationships, and positively impacting company profits. In addition, I've demonstrated my ongoing interest in sales through my community service, which includes personally raising $28k for local charities over the last five years. As Keropac expands, I'm *confident my background will be an asset to the sales team, and welcome the chance to be part of this exciting growth period.*

Thank you for your consideration. I look forward to further sharing how I can make a positive contribution to Keropac, and will contact you next week to answer any questions you might have about the materials I have submitted.

Sincerely,

Patricia Simon

Some final tips:

- **Drop the ego.** Be careful of overusing the words "I," "me," and "my," especially at the beginning of sentences.
- **Show your personality.** A cover letter allows for more freedom to be creative than you have in the resume itself. Allow your personality and energy to come through so the letter is more engaging.
- **Avoid disclosing salary requirements.** If asked in the application, state that your salary expectations are "aligned with current market rates for similar roles."
- **Address the letter to a specific person.** If you're unable to find a name, "Dear Hiring Team" is acceptable.

Social Media (It's *Not* Optional)

In a job search, not being on social media is the equivalent of not existing. Yes, there's always that outlier, but they're becoming increasingly rare. Without an online presence, your search will be harder. You could schedule a lesson with your teenager on how to use Snapchat, Instagram, and the app du jour, but that's unnecessary. At minimum, you need to have a well-developed profile on a reputable professional site like LinkedIn. Plenty of books and online resources can help you create a polished professional profile for social media. I'll cover a few things critical to Switchers, specifically how you can rebrand to align with your Plan A, even if you don't yet have a lot of related experience.

SWITCH ACTION

Rebrand Your Social Media Profile

YOU CAN'T CHANGE YOUR past, but you can revisit your professional social media profiles to make sure every element is consistent with your new brand and advances your Plan A.

Google Yourself!

THE INTERNET HOUSES INFINITE data, and it's all fair game in the job search process, for both you as a job seeker and hirers looking to minimize risk. If you haven't Googled yourself in a while (or ever), now is a perfect time—preferably on a computer other than your own, which has "stored memory" that may make it less objective. It's in your best interest to know what information is available about you online—chances are, a good portion might not have been posted by you.

Yes, your LinkedIn profile and personal website should pop up at the top of a Google search, but you'll also likely find data related to public records ("My future employer can see how much I paid for my house?"), conferences you attended ("I forgot I was on that guest panel . . ."), organized volunteer events you participated in ("881st place in the charity triathlon? Not bad!"), and social events that you attended ("Whoa, I ruled the dance floor at that wedding!"). Some of the information connected to you might not even be about *you* but rather someone who shares your name. This happens a lot if you have a common name, and a recruiter may not search carefully enough to learn that the DUI mug shot isn't actually yours.

If do you find an old fraternity photo posted by your college roommate that doesn't reflect your best, what can you do? You should reach out to the website owner and have it removed, but the photo may have been copied to other sites. When you're unable to remove information, piling positive information on top of it is your next best bet. This also works if you find that many of the search results relate to your former brand. Now is a perfect time to create a personal website that can layer over old search data. Recruiters will dig, but they are busy, and if they find enough favorable information they're not likely to go much further. If the questionable information is about someone who shares your name, consider giving the hirer a heads-up as you move through the process.

Update Your LinkedIn Profile

LINKEDIN HAS BEEN THE premiere social media site for job seekers for over a decade. Having a well-groomed, brand-aligned, completed profile on LinkedIn is *core* to your job search. So if you're not on the site or haven't revisited your profile in a while, do it now. Even the least diligent hiring managers will review your LinkedIn page. If it's obvious you're not active—you have few connections, limited or outdated information, a missing headshot—it's a red flag. If you want to be in the game, you must play ball. Because specifications and functionality are updated regularly, check out the many books, articles, and online tutorials for the latest advice on how to optimize your LinkedIn profile. Learn how to use the site to connect with new contacts, to research companies, and to find critical information for your networking meetings, interviews, and even salary negotiation. LinkedIn is much more than a glorified Rolodex in the job search. It's worth investing in.

Put Your Online Presence to Work

AS A SWITCHER, THERE are several things you can do online to shift your brand from the old to the new. You can build a personal website that demonstrates your skills and passion for your Plan A. This is low-cost and simple with the templates available. Harvey wanted to focus on a job in marketing after twenty years running operations in a local golf course and entertainment center, so he put his technology skills to work and created a personal website that highlighted his skills related to marketing, including his web-design abilities.

You can also create a blog that centers around a core topic in your new field—or, if that feels too audacious, follow industry leaders in your target field and repost their work adding your insightful comments for others to view. This will likely get you noticed by the original blog poster as well—bonus! You can join online forums, comment or respond to questions posted on sites like Quora, podcast, record short videos, or create infographics or other creative media to get noticed. The technology keeps expanding.

I understand that some of these ideas are intimidating, especially because you don't yet consider yourself an expert in your newly chosen field. Just remember that everyone begins *someplace*, and your online presence is a key step on the way to communicating your new brand. You likely know more than you think and, at a minimum, people will be impressed by your passion and courage. Find the medium that feels most comfortable for you and try it. Making a switch isn't easy, and this is one of those areas that makes Switchers successful.

IN SUMMARY

Familiar job search tools, such as resumes, were designed with traditional candidates in mind. But if you follow the advice in this chapter, you will be head and shoulders above the competition.

Why? Because many traditional candidates don't put as much work into these documents and tools as you will. You'd be surprised how many applicants wing it, especially traditional candidates who believe they can get by on a history of similar jobs. It's obvious when a job seeker is simply papering the internet with applications to see what sticks. A Switcher doesn't have that luxury, and your effort alone will win you points.

In the end, it likely won't be the cover letter that gets you hired or your social media that enables you to be found by a recruiter. But don't cut any corners. Details matter, and sometimes what you *don't* say or write speaks volumes.

CHAPTER SEVEN SWITCH POINTS

→ The most interesting and sought-after jobs are scooped up quickly through referrals and rarely make it to the big job boards. Networking is your best entrée into a company if you want to find the good roles and reduce your competition.

→ A hirer will spend about six seconds reviewing your resume before making an initial decision. Ensure you end up in the "yes" pile by creating a results-based, well-formatted resume that makes it easy for the reader to quickly discern your relevant strengths.

→ Include a cover letter. This will set you apart from the pack and is another opportunity to reiterate your relevant strengths, career story, and value.

→ Social media isn't optional. Make sure your brand comes through clearly in your online presence, and remove irrelevant or inappropriate content.

→ Few things in life are truly "have to's." When you choose to do something, it is a lot more empowering.

IV

Create
Ambassadors

No Excuses

Your Network Really Is
Your Net Worth

I've put a lot of emphasis on networking and for good reason. A network is the most important tool in the job search arsenal, and it's especially true for Switchers. But the idea of networking can be daunting. What does *networking* even mean, and how the heck do you get started? In this chapter, we'll look at what networking really is and how to do it effectively. Maybe you'll even enjoy it (maybe . . .). As you work through this chapter, you will:

- Gain a better understanding of what networking truly consists of
- Become a more confident networker
- Learn how to get started if you don't have a large network
- Get helpful advice on how to make networking easier if you're an introvert
- Complete an exercise to create time in your schedule for networking

But I Don't Know Anyone

According to the laws of aviation, bumblebees shouldn't be able to fly. Scientists have concluded their bodies are too heavy for their wingspan, and that flying is aerodynamically unfeasible. Since bumblebees don't know about this physical limitation, they fly perfectly fine. We can achieve a lot when our mind doesn't pay attention to supposed limitations. This works for your perceived networking limitations also. Many people envision a network as some inaccessible group of super-connected professionals who have available jobs falling out of their pockets. But it's much simpler than that. A network is a group of people you have relationships with, and "relationship" is the key word. Your current network consists of family, friends, neighbors, colleagues, or classmates. The good news is that everyone already has a network. You may simply need to e-x-p-a-n-d it, which is less daunting than starting fresh.

The purpose of a network is to link you to people who have information or resources that can help you to reach a goal, usually via people you already know. Imagine the wide trunk of an oak tree with large branches that separate into smaller ones until they offshoot to twigs. In this analogy, you are the trunk and your network is all the branches, with the largest being the strongest connections (family, friends, close colleagues) and the twigs being

distant connections (former coworkers, friends of friends, acquaintances you met in passing, high school classmates on Facebook). When you think about it this way, you may realize your network is larger than you thought, which is a positive first step. You already know lots of people.

So you have a network. Now what? Whether you're looking for a new job or a reliable mechanic, networking works the same way:

- Meet and establish the relationship.
- Build trust over time through repeated interactions.
- Exchange mutually beneficial information and resources.
- Ask for help with something this person is qualified to assist with and reciprocate when possible.

Networking can be straightforward. If your neighbor is a car enthusiast, you'd ask her to recommend a good mechanic when your brakes need repairs. Want to eat at a great Italian restaurant? Ask your foodie colleague. Need a reliable dog sitter? Ask the guy down the street with two Standard Poodles. You likely network regularly without realizing it. But yes, the stakes are higher when you're looking for a job, and most people in your inner circle won't have an instant recommendation. This is where second-level contacts come in. Second-level contacts are not in your immediate network; rather they are people *your* network contacts know. Second-level contacts are pivotal to your search, so we'll revisit this group frequently.

Research shows that second-level contacts are more effective in a job search than first-level contacts, because they have access to information that you do not.[1] So your goal is to engage the relationships you have already established to get to your second-level and third-level contacts. We'll explore accessing your second-level contacts in Chapter Nine. First, it's time to put your networking concerns to rest.

Get Your Life Back in 15 Minutes

Responsibility—Reality—Risk—Resilience

IF I EARNED A dime for every time I heard someone say "I don't have time," I could retire early.

I'm guilty, too. The truth is, we spend our time exactly how we want. Although we prefer to rationalize that we don't have a choice, we always do. While I may not convince you to leave the office earlier or skip that rerun of *Law & Order* so you can network, I have a little trick that allows me to accomplish more each day, with hardly any change to my life. On our daily to-do list, we typically have two general types of tasks:

- Lengthy tasks that take an hour or more, such as going to the gym, cleaning the garage, writing an article, or completing a work project.
- Quick tasks that take less than 15 minutes, such as scheduling a haircut, responding to an email, paying a bill, or setting up a meeting.

Coincidentally, throughout the day, our chunks of time typically fall into two general buckets:

- Large chunks of time of an hour or more—perhaps before your spouse gets home, after the kids go to bed, or early on Saturday mornings.
- Small chunks of time of about 15 minutes, such as before a meeting starts, while you're waiting for dinner to cook, or during your commute on the train.

When we have time (either large or small chunks), our tendency is to get the quick tasks completed first, because they're easy, and give us a sense of accomplishment. We can check something off the list—woo hoo! The problem is that we end up using 60- to 90-minute chunks of time to call the dentist, check email, and scan Facebook instead of working out or tackling the mess in the garage. Then, when we have a 15-minute period of time before dinner, we have already completed our quick tasks for the day.

The trick is simple. As you begin your day, identify 15-minute tasks and match them up with your 15-minute chunks of time. Save your hour-plus chunks of time for the lengthy tasks. Why not try this trick for a week? You may be surprised at how much you accomplish in the same 24 hours per day that you had last week.

I'm Not a Good Networker

We can boil networking down to the idea of forming mutually beneficial relationships. You've built many of those over your life and career, so most people are "good at networking" in the basic sense. But in a job search, networking takes on a new meaning and suddenly seems awkward and difficult. There's a lot more at stake when you are looking for a job than when you're trying to find a decent restaurant. Many of us associate our job with our identity (see Chapter Two), so we may feel more vulnerable in a job search.

So simply forget about asking for a job. It isn't really what networking is about, and most people you speak with won't have one to offer anyway. Instead, begin meeting new people to gather information. Ask questions, be curious, and share experiences. Have *conversations*. Form human connections. Here are some examples of my favorite general conversation starters:

- What do you love about what you do?
- What has surprised you about your profession (or company)?
- In the news, I recently saw [insert non-controversial current event]. How does this impact your field?

That is networking, so you likely are better at it than you think. No more excuses. I know this doesn't get you a job . . . yet. But it's how relationships form. We'll get into the mechanics of strategic networking later, but for now, recognize that you already have all the skills to build relationships.

Networking?
Where the Heck Do I Start?

This is the million-dollar question, but it's really not so overwhelming. Here's the answer. Start with the companies you're targeting. You need a structure that is easy to follow and track. In Chapter Seven, we talked about the pitfalls of a "reactive" job search and why it's a futile approach for the Switcher. A proactive approach provides structure and makes your search more effective. Here's the process I recommend:

1. **Start with the companies.** Research the types of companies (industries, culture, geography, size) that interest you based on your Plan A. Make a list of 20 or more actual organizations that meet these criteria. Reach beyond the top names like Google and Goldman Sachs. As of 2012, more than 99.7 percent of U.S. organizations had fewer than 500 employees, which means you have lots of options that you don't yet know about.[2] Find them! Look at LinkedIn or other professional websites, your local biz journal, Forbes.com's "Best Companies to Work For" list, *Inc. Magazine*'s "500 Fastest Growing" list, and similar resources. Steve Dalton's book *The 2-Hour Job Search* offers great advice to help you do this.[3]

2. **Uncover your current contacts.** Use your connections on professional networking sites to identify first- and second-level contacts who are currently (or were previously) employed at

companies you're targeting. It may be tougher to find connections at smaller companies, but don't let that stop you. The internet holds a wealth of information, so if you can't find a contact, search for the company name and the word "recruiter" to see what you can uncover. Engage your sleuthing skills and you'll be surprised how many direct names you find. Don't allow fear to get in your way! If it were easy, everyone would do it. Successful Switchers plough through doubt to get what they want. You can, too!

3. **Start the conversation.** Reach out to your current contacts to relay interest in learning more about their company. If you only find a second-level contact at a company in your LinkedIn search, ask the first-level connection for an introduction. Not sure what to say? See Chapter Nine for sample scripts.

4. **Get creative.** No connections? No problem. If you can find the company on a professional networking site like LinkedIn, search the profiles of current employees, and find something you have in common with them. Perhaps you went to the same university, follow similar Thought Leaders, or support a shared cause. Use this as an entry point to introduce yourself. Being proactive takes a little courage. But, if you don't ask, the answer is always "no." You have nothing to lose and everything to gain.

5. **Stay in touch.** Networking is about cultivating a relationship over several contact points and building a mutually beneficial partnership. Approach your contacts from a standpoint of exploration and curiosity. Don't push your resume on them. Be proactive, but allow the relationship to develop naturally. Soon you'll get introductions to others inside the companies that you're targeting. Patience and diplomatic persistence are key.

We'll cover the "how" of networking in greater depth in the next chapter. For now, it's important to have an approach you feel comfortable following, with a solid point to begin from.

You already have a network to draw on, you have the skills to grow your network further, and you even have a process to follow. But networking still may not feel comfortable or easy to work into your schedule. If that's the case, keep reading!

"Networking Feels Dirty," says Science

If your objection to networking is that you hate schmoozing, it's time to reframe how you think about it. In his book *Give and Take*, Adam Grant highlights three types of professional interaction styles—givers, matchers, and takers[4]—and if you fall into the last bucket, it's no wonder you dislike networking. You're doing it wrong! Takers have a one-way "I'll do it if it benefits me" approach, whereas effective networking is a two-way relationship that builds over time. When done with positive intentions and just as much interest in giving as getting, it actually feels satisfying. Forming connections for *mutual* gain is legitimately networking.

However, if you feel a little gross about it, you're not alone— studies show that networking literally makes people feel dirty.[5] But the *reason* people in those studies felt dirty was that the relationships were one-sided. So, yes, if you're a "taker" using someone purely for your own personal career gain, you should feel icky. If you're not, but you still feel guilty, chances are you're uncomfortable being vulnerable. This does feel scary. No one likes rejection. However, you cannot let it stand in your way. Keep this advice in mind:

☞ More than 70 percent of people find jobs through networking, at one time or another, so *everyone* seeks out advice for their career advancement.[6] This is *your* time. Who knows when your contacts will next be in a job search and reach out to you?

☞ You may have nothing to offer in return for someone's time or connections right now, but that time will come. Remember the generosity of others, and strive to return the favor.[7] If you cannot, then pay it forward to others. Generosity begets generosity.

☞ Networking is *not* about asking for a job. In fact, in most of your networking meetings, you'll talk about people, projects, the market, companies, and the like. If you end up speaking about an actual job, you're not networking . . . you're interviewing (and that could be great, too)!

Who Has Time to Network?

You may think you can't possibly squeeze networking events into your already full calendar, but remember: We all make time for whatever we *most* want to do. If you truly want to pursue a career switch, you will find time—even if it's painful to say "no" elsewhere. Not convinced? Try the following exercise.

SWITCH ACTION

Find Time to Network

FOR AN ENTIRE WEEK, track how you use your time. Include everything professional and personal. Include little stuff like hitting snooze, checking email, scanning social media, watching reruns, chatting by the coffee maker, looking for flights to Aruba, and texting friends. You'll be shocked to discover all the hidden pockets of time available to you.

Allot some of this time for networking: Send an email to a new (or old) acquaintance, post a comment on social media, or pass along a job opening to a former colleague. There is always time, you just need to *choose* to spend it working toward your goal. Can you think of a better way to use time than reaching for your dream job?

Also, scheduling an activity increases the likelihood that you'll do it.[8] So *add* networking to your calendar. Schedule one lunch with a contact, one coffee meeting, 15 minutes checking industry-specific information, and so on. Block the time. You can only benefit, and small, consistent actions add up and lead to awesome outcomes. Try it and see!

Introversion Is *Not* a Flaw

If you're an introvert, you might feel like you're just not cut out for networking. The introversion–extroversion personality trait has gotten a lot of attention in recent years, thanks to books like Susan Cain's *Quiet*.[9] For introverts, time spent with others, particularly in large groups, depletes their energy, whereas time spent alone replenishes it. Note that introversion is different from shyness, which is "a lack of confidence in social situations."[10] I'm an introvert and so I'm happiest staying at home with an interesting book or eating lunch at my desk. While recharge time is legitimately necessary, I realized several years ago it's possible to miss out on professional opportunities by prioritizing time alone over cultivating my network. Don't make the same mistake.

There are many ways to network, and not all of them require you to be in a room full of strangers making small talk. Find what works for you. Perhaps you're comfortable with one-on-one meetings, or maybe you enjoy meeting people with common professional or personal interests. Experiment. You may never *love* networking, but once you experience the many benefits, the uncomfortable moments will become worth it!

While walking into a large room bustling with people is still not my idea of a fun time, I've developed strategies to network comfortably and effectively in crowded events. I do need recharge time afterward, but usually enjoy the conversations and always learn something worthwhile. Here are my favorite strategies:

☞ **Get a wingman.** It's easy to find a reason to skip a networking event (traffic is ridiculous, I have laundry to do). I seem to find critical things to do when I'm supposed to be attending a big social event. Having a wingman can help to get to the event, which is half the battle. Just be sure to split up and meet new people instead of solely chatting with one another. You can share your new connections to double the return.

☞ **Use your strengths.** As pointed out in Chapter Six, many people find talking about themselves to be more satisfying than money, and introverts tend to be excellent listeners. So, if you're getting antsy at an event, do what you do best: Listen and allow others to talk. Have a list of open-ended questions to ask people, and give them time to answer. If you are genuinely interested, there can be an instant connection.

☞ **Plan a transition moment.** Genetic research has shown, "it takes introverts longer than extroverts to reconstitute themselves when they are depleted."[11] If you're attending an event after a crazy day at work and a hectic commute, take a quiet minute for yourself in your car or in the restroom before entering. These mini-recharge moments can boost your energy.

☞ **Take on a role.** Introverts feel more comfortable in crowds when they have a designated role, whether it's helping people sign in or handing out name tags. It gives you an instant icebreaker and a reason to meet people. If you don't have an official role, observe how you might pitch in and ask the organizer if he'd like a hand. Large events are always in need of people to help with handouts or give attendees directions to the coatroom.

☞ **Have an entry and exit strategy.** Breaking into or making a graceful exit from a discussion can be challenging. Groups of three or more are usually easier to join than pairs, so start there. A simple "Can I join you?" is all it takes. When you're ready to move on, ask for a business card or graciously state, "It was great to meet you." Don't overthink it—simplicity works best. Excusing yourself to refill your drink or use the restroom also works. Continuing to circulate benefits everyone.

☞ **Ditch the pitch.** Yes, it's important to share key information about yourself, but the "elevator pitch" is not a useful way to begin a relationship. Former Harvard professor Amy Cuddy's research shows it's more important to be perceived as trustworthy first, and only then is someone interested in your level of competence. In the caveman days, it was more important to survival to allow a person into the tribe who could be trusted not to steal the harvest than one who could hunt.[12] So, be human, not a talking billboard. Curiosity and an interesting question—"What do you enjoy most about your field?"—can go a long way. Starting an engaging conversation (not getting a job) should be your primary goal. Have a few key aspects of your BVP ready to convey, but be conversational. Share sound bites that invite questions and don't stress about how you're coming across. If this is the first meeting, it's most important to be likable, curious, and interested so that you get to the second meeting.

☞ **Find your peeps.** Researchers have estimated that up to 50 percent of attendees at any networking event also find it uncomfortable to engage new people.[13] Scan for people standing on their own (and most likely buried in their smartphones in today's culture). They'll likely be delighted you approached them, and a simple statement about the event can be the perfect icebreaker ("Hi, I'm Dawn. This is my first regional conference. Have you been to these before?"). After a few minutes, keep circulating or invite other "soloists" to join your growing group.

Don't sell yourself short. Extroverts may be more comfortable networking, but that doesn't mean they are any more *effective* at it.[14] Building new relationships is a completely different skill and, regardless of personality, it's a skill you can learn.

IN SUMMARY

When it comes to networking, most people have more excuses than strategies. Energy that could be spent growing connections is often wasted belaboring the reasons why it doesn't make sense to reach out, or why it would be better to wait, or why those contacts probably couldn't help anyway. It's true that not everyone will return your call. Not every conversation will move you closer to your goal. Sometimes it might take months or years before you see the fruits of your labor. But the more you work at it, the more likely you'll reap the benefits. Like most things, you get out what you put in.

If you're still waffling about networking, my question is, "So what happens in your job search if you *don't* reach out?" The answer is invariably "nothing." You won't form more relationships, you won't get interesting information about the company you're targeting, you won't get introductions or referrals, and you won't be one step closer to landing that job switch. When you look at it that way, the trade-off seems well worth the risk.

Networking becomes infinitely more comfortable over time. Your network is your net worth, and the people who find success aren't simply in the right place at the right time. Rather, they've invested in meeting the right *people* so they continuously access opportunities that others miss. Luck is what happens when preparation meets networking!

CHAPTER EIGHT SWITCH POINTS

→ You've likely been networking all your life. Recall the people you know and the relationship skills you've gained. Networking is networking, whether you're looking for a job or an authentic Italian restaurant.

→ You need to network to make a career switch. Stop making excuses, and put energy and time into building mutually beneficial relationships.

→ Second- (and third-) level connections are where the action is! Most people in your immediate circle have the same information you do, so the goal is to get to *their* network, because that is where your next opportunity lies.

→ Introversion is not a flaw, and it certainly doesn't make you bad at networking. Find strategies that are comfortable, engage your strengths, and build relationships.

→ Use your 24 hours each day wisely and don't waste large chunks of time on 15-minute tasks.

• • • • • • • • • • • •

The New Way to Network

Create Ambassadors

In Chapter Eight, we talked about how critical networking is to a successful job switch. But all the networking in the world won't get you far if you don't have a strategy. In the sections that follow, I'll show you the best ways to network so your contacts walk away impressed, informed, and eager to help you in your career switch. In this chapter, you will learn:

- Why second-level contacts are your best assets when it comes to networking
- How to reach out to first-level contacts you've fallen out of touch with
- How to turn your contacts into ambassadors
- How to use the GLIDE strategy for killer networking meetings
- What else you can do to make sure you're head and shoulders above the competition for your contacts' assistance
- Strategies to overcome bouts of impostor syndrome

Networking Gold: Second-Level Contacts

In 1973, a Stanford sociologist published a paper that several decades later would unknowingly be the foundation for the social media–based job search. Mark S. Granovetter recognized that, at a very basic level, "weak ties" (connections to people we interact with infrequently and are not as intimately engaged with) tend to be the bridges to information that we might not have access to through our "strong ties" (those people with whom we have close relationships, that is, our close first-level contacts).[1] The premise is that people closest to us travel in the same circles we do and have access to similar information. However, weak ties access different people and information, so when we connect with them, new circles open to us.

Eva was in a corporate role, and was looking for a similar position in the education field (industry Switcher). She had completed many online applications, but hadn't been contacted yet. Her boyfriend (first-level contact) worked with a woman (second-level contact) who was married to the vice provost of a local university (third-level contact). Eva's boyfriend spoke with his colleague, who happily passed Eva's resume on to her husband, and a week later she was contacted for a phone interview.

When you're networking for a new job, weak ties are critical. Your strong ties (such as your family and close friends) likely don't have jobs to hand out, or you'd already know about them. Weak ties, including college classmates or coworkers from three jobs ago, are more likely to bring you novel information. And their contacts (your second-level contacts), such as your yoga buddy's spouse or your hairstylist's other client, may be the people who will introduce you to your next boss (a third-level contact). This is awesome news for Switchers. You already have a vast network.

Warm Up Cold Contacts

On social media you already have many contacts who can be bridges to your next opportunity via weak ties. The only thing you need to do is reach out to warm the relationship. Here are some ways to do that.

Do a Network Inventory

Identify first-level contacts who have gone cold and find their most recent contact information. Cast your net wide: Look at people you've texted or emailed over the last few years, scroll through social media feeds, peruse your online alumni database, and review your calendar appointments. Make a list of these contacts, and organize it by company, specialty, or location. Catch up on recent events in your contacts' lives through social media. This will be useful when you reach out.

Reestablish Relationships That Have Gone Cold

When you get back in touch with your weak ties to reestablish the connection, your first communication should *not* be a request. Relationships are built on mutual benefit and generosity, so offer something helpful like passing along an interesting tidbit or a pleasantry such as a note of congratulations on a recent marriage or promotion. If this isn't feasible, a friendly "Hello Karin, it's been a while. I see you've moved back East. How is your summer going?" will suffice. Open the door to a conversation and see where it leads. If you're considerate, chances are your contact will do her best to help later, even just in the spirit of good networking.

Be Gracious and Flexible

When you're in a job search, it's *your* top priority. But it's *not* the priority of others, and although your contacts may wish to help, it might be a busy time for them. If your email goes unanswered, wait two weeks and try again. If you're truly interested in reestablishing the relationship (not just seeing if this person can be useful to you now, which is a "taker" approach), then you'll make it a priority. If you only reach out when you need something, fewer and fewer people will respond.

Keep Your Network Simmering

Once you reestablish your connections, prevent your network from going cold again, as it'll be harder to warm it up a second time. Technology and social media provide ways to stay connected easily. Set calendar reminders for friends' and colleagues' birthdays, create an industry-focused newsletter or blog for interested parties, write one recommendation or testimonial per month for someone, or endorse, "like," and share content that others produce. Develop a sustainable strategy and use it. You'll be glad you did.

SWITCH ACTION

Reconnecting with Contacts That Have Gone Cold

WHY NOT START REVITALIZING your contact list today? Reach out to someone from your past with the sole purpose of reestablishing the connection. To get you started, here are a couple of sample scripts for common situations that will help you to build your connections via email or on professional networking sites.

Sample #1

Hi Michelle! How are you? I noticed on social media you've changed jobs and are now a Senior Buyer at Top Retail, Inc. Congratulations—what an achievement! I'd love to catch up and hear more about it. How's everything? Things are well with me. The summer flew by and I'm starting to consider some potential career changes of my own. All the best in the new job and please let me know when you'll be downtown so we can connect. Warmly, Susie

Sample #2

Hi Matt, it's been a while! I came across your profile on LinkedIn and wanted to send an invite to connect. It looks like things are going well—Senior Manager, eh? Well done and well deserved! Let's catch up soon. I'll be flying through Chicago next month and would welcome meeting for coffee if you're game. See you soon! Michael

Sample #3

Hey Gerry—how have you been? You'll never guess who I ran into at the reunion last week—Jen! It reminded me of when we all worked together on the R&D team. Let me know if you're up for grabbing a drink after work sometime—we can reminisce about our days at Scientifica. Best, Steve

When you reach out to one person a day for a week, you may be surprised at how many new circles you'll create from your weak ties in your first-level contacts. Once the momentum begins, you'll start to see results in the form of information, contacts, and leads. Reestablishing these connections may expose opportunities you would otherwise never have access to, so why not dive in now?

The Ask

I used to be on the Board of Directors for an amazing nonprofit, and although I thoroughly believed in the mission, I dreaded "the ask"—that necessary task of requesting donations. But without funding, there wouldn't be an organization, so I experimented until I found a method that felt comfortable for me. As you start to strengthen your contact list, you'll need to do the same regarding your networking.

Whether you're reaching out to re-warmed contacts, friends, or complete strangers, asking for help can be intimidating. Saying hello or sending a congratulatory note is a great first step, but if you don't eventually ask for assistance, you'll spend your life drinking lots of coffee at networking meetings with nothing to show except a serious caffeine buzz. To get you started, I've provided some sample scripts for common situations that will help you to craft a concise and professional email to request assistance.

SWITCH ACTION

Sample Scripts for Common Networking Situations

Reaching Out to Request an Introduction
to One of Their Contacts (Second-Level Contacts)

Use this when you know the person well enough to ask for a "warm" introduction to someone in their circle.

Hi Carina, how are you? Are you all settled in the new house? Things are going well at Colonia Partners—however, after six years it's time to start considering other companies where I can grow my skills. Medtronic is a company I'm pursuing and through my research on LinkedIn, I noticed you're connected to Danielle Bishop who works there. Would you be willing to make an introduction? I'd love to learn more about Medtronic and gain insight into the culture. Much thanks—hope your Fall is off to a great start! Best, Amy

Reaching Out Directly to Second-Level Contacts with Whom You Share a Common Contact or Interest

Use this when you don't know the mutual connection well enough to ask for a "warm" introduction to your second-level contact or when the commonality you share is an alma mater, former employer, etc.

Hi Katie, we've never met, but have a mutual contact in common—Rhonda Nolan at Vanguard. Your profile came up when I was doing research on Lane Health Systems. Given your background there, I was wondering if you might be willing to connect for 15 minutes via phone to share your insights on the company as I'm very interested in learning more. Currently, I'm a project manager at Vance Insurance, and am planning to make a transition to the healthcare industry in the next six months. Any suggestions would be greatly appreciated. Thank you in advance for your time. Warmly, Kyle

Reaching Out to a Contact "Cold"

Use this when you find someone on social media or through other means but are unable to find a mutual connection or commonality:

Dear James, we've not met, but I found your contact information while researching financial leaders on LinkedIn. I have worked in capital markets for eight years and am looking to move to the other side of the business. Your profile caught my eye because you seem to have made that switch during your career. If you would be open to a 15-minute phone call, I'd love to understand your strategy for making the change and any surprises you encountered. Please let me know if there is a convenient time. Thank you, Alanna

Not everyone will respond, even when you try one more time after two weeks. Some contacts will reply with the trite "Send me your resume and I'll pass it around" response. Be careful—this is often a dead end, an empty offer that is a polite way to excuse themselves from the situation. If there is an actual, relevant job opening in their company, yes, send your resume to them to forward to human resources or better yet, the hiring manager. If not, reply "Thanks for that generous offer—I will certainly take you up on it at the appropriate time. However, what would be most helpful now would be an introduction to the manager who heads up the Accounting Department." For a more in-depth overview on how to "read" your networking audience and how helpful they might be, check out Steve Dalton's discussion about Curmudgeons, Obligates, and Boosters in *The 2-Hour Job Search*.[2]

Remember that networking is a *process,* not an event. Don't get frustrated because you expect efforts to produce instant results, when it's really about planting seeds, nurturing relationships, and giving things time to pan out. You may not see the benefits of networking for months, sometimes years, so it's important to always be networking to keep contacts and the flow of information fresh. Contacts you make today might pave the path to your *next* job change, five years from now. A lack of immediate results doesn't mean your networking isn't working.

Making Second-Level Contacts *First*-Level

Most candidates know that asking for a job in an initial networking meeting is the equivalent of asking for your crush's hand in marriage on the first date, but many people still subconsciously approach networking with this "one and done" mentality. While not every contact will end up being a friend, most people have *something* to offer if you listen carefully and are curious. And remember, you never know who *their* contacts are (second-level contacts!).

One of those potential second-level contacts might turn out to be vital to your next job. So, if you find that your networking efforts with new people aren't establishing relationships, incorporate strategies that make it easier to stay in touch.

If the first meeting went well, ask permission to follow up in a specified period of time that is appropriate for your next steps:

☞ "Thank you, Pat, this has been very helpful. If it's okay, I'll reach out next month after the new budget in your Regional planning meeting is set to see where things stand for the restructuring project that we talked about."

Or, if your contact made a suggestion, follow up with her after you've implemented it:

☞ "Hi Rosann, I wanted to let you know you were right—the AMA convention was a perfect place to meet like-minded professionals and I now have some fantastic leads. Thank you again for recommending that I attend. I'll keep you posted on how things turn out. In the meantime, I hope your upcoming travels go well."

Another strategy is asking your new contact to introduce you to someone in her network:

☞ "This has been great, Maggie—I really appreciate your time and have gained a lot of insight through hearing about your experiences. Something that caught my attention was the global expansion project you mentioned. Is there someone on your team you might recommend I speak with to learn more about this?"

If you're able to search professional networking sites and get the name of a specific person among your new connections *prior* to your meeting, that's even better. You'll gain points by doing the work for them. (Note: Engage this strategy prudently only if the initial meeting went well.)

☛ "Paula, I can't thank you enough for your time this morning. After hearing about your experience with the company, I'm even more excited to pursue opportunities there in the upcoming months. On LinkedIn, I noticed you're connected to Laura Giorge in the Marketing Department. Is she someone you would feel comfortable introducing me to?"

Superconnector is a term used to describe individuals who connect their networking *circles* through introductions. As the common link between the initial two connections, the superconnector stays top of mind in both circles, which creates a triangulation effect that exponentially expands your network over time.

☛ "Dear Ford, I wanted to tell you how helpful our conversation was a few weeks ago. It occurred to me that my former colleague Carrie has her own social media marketing business and might have interesting ideas on how to publicize your upcoming book. I've included her website below and would be happy to make an introduction."

When someone invests in you, always send a thank-you email, and if you're not already connected, reach out on professional social media with a personalized invitation to connect within 48 hours:

☛ "Dear Sue, It was great speaking with you on Thursday at the AMA convention. Thank you for sharing your insights about Bain & Co., and I look forward to staying in touch. Please let me know if your travels bring you through Philadelphia. I'd love to buy you a WaWa coffee!"

When you meet a new business contact, remember the goal is building the relationship so you "get to the second date" and create a new first-level contact in your network. That's when trust develops and more valuable information is shared, so avoid the "one and done" mentality and build something meaningful by following up in ways like these:

☞ **Engage technology.** LinkedIn can do the heavy lifting on reminders about work anniversaries, birthdays, new jobs, and promotions. It can help you celebrate your contacts' wins. Browse notifications daily—just five minutes can make a difference.

☞ **Attend events.** If your contacts will be congregating at a conference, retirement party, or happy hour, make it a point to go. A few minutes of face time can go a long way.

☞ **Give thanks.** We accomplish nothing alone. When you have a "win," reach out to those who helped you achieve it, no matter how small their role.

☞ **Contribute on social media.** Promote your contact's speaking engagement, offer a tip, share a friend's job opening. With technology, we're all able to be thought leaders, and sharing relevant content keeps you in front of your network.

Why Create Ambassadors?

The research on networking has been consistent for decades—it's the strongest path to job opportunities, hands down. But if I could, I would do away with the word "networking" as it relates to the job search and call it "creating ambassadors" instead. Because the key isn't just *who* you know, but also *what they* know about you and their brand experience with you. You can have one million connections around the world, but if none are willing or know how to advocate for you, then it won't matter. If you're "networking like crazy" in your career transition and it's still not creating results, you're probably having a lot of interactions, but *not* creating ambassadors.

Having ambassadors in a variety of circles significantly helps you expand your knowledge and opportunities. Realize that once a new contact has a clear understanding of your brand and what you are looking for, he or she can scan the environment for opportunities that are a good fit. So contacts can be out in the world bringing helpful information back to you. After all, you can't be *everywhere*.

Turning Contacts into Ambassadors

The best way to create ambassadors is to focus on the relationship, *not* the outcome. To turn a contact into an ambassador, you must make sure the person with whom you're meeting:

- Clearly understands your Brand Value Proposition (BVP) and target (Plan A)
- Forms a favorable impression of you that they can relay clearly to others

Otherwise, how or why would they introduce you to their contacts or even stay in touch? Think about what impresses *you* when you meet someone. You probably notice the person is prepared, asks intelligent questions, is curious and engaged, shares common interests, has interesting perspectives, and is positive. A networking meeting isn't about spewing your credentials and skills onto your unsuspecting contact until her eyes glaze. Instead, select two accomplishments to share that illustrate your Plan A and the value you bring, then focus on learning about your new acquaintance. In the words of Dale Carnegie, "You can make more friends in two months by becoming interested in other people than you can in two years by trying to get other people interested in you."[3]

Do the Work for Your Contacts— You'll Earn Major Points!

Don't ask contacts, "What do you think I should do?" This is an amateur blunder. You'll appear unprepared and unprofessional. No one except you is qualified to answer that question, and asking contacts to do the groundwork for you is disrespectful. They are being gracious with their time, not doing the heavy lifting. Do the work for them by giving contacts the language to use to sell you to *their* contacts. Don't leave this up to chance and assume they'll take the time or have the right information to summarize your brand and convince a third party that you're worth talking to. Create an ambassador by doing this work for them!

For example, compare these two statements:

1. "I'm really passionate about logistics and love to travel, so I'm thinking my next role should be with a company that's expanding its global operations."

2. "After three tours in Iraq, I understand both the criticality and difficulty of effectively forecasting and coordinating the movement of supplies across global lines. With little room for error and rigid timelines, I've learned how to nimbly negotiate and influence according to local customs and use sophisticated algorithms to predict the best pathways to ship goods efficiently. This is why I'm interested in Worldwide Renewables, Corp."

Which one would persuade *you* to tell your Global Supply Chain Director about this person? Your contacts aren't that concerned with what you're "passionate about." The second statement assures your contacts know that you're both motivated *and* qualified, while giving them the language to sell you to others. It also gives them confidence they can recommend you without worrying it will reflect poorly on them. While no method is guaranteed, when you do the work for your network, your return on investment will skyrocket.

GLIDE Questions
(The New Way to Network)

To captivate your audience and turn them into ambassadors, you need to be unique, concise, and impressive. (Note: Being impressive has less to do with past experiences and more to do with confidence, preparation, and follow-through.) It's unlikely you'll get more than 20 minutes to chat with a new contact, and it'll probably be over the phone initially, so the message you communicate must be compelling, attention-getting, clear, logical, and genuine. That's a tall order for 20 minutes!

If you pull it off, you'll stand out from the others who are vying for your contact's attention. While you may not get to communicate everything you want in the first meeting or ask all your questions, that's fine, because the goal of the *first* meeting is always to get to a *second* meeting. One of the best ways to turn contacts into ambassadors is to be polite and respectful of their time. Avoid uninspired questions like "What should I do next?" "What is the market outlook?" or "How can I get into this field?" They not only put your contact on the spot, but also demonstrate you haven't done your part to prepare. If you can find the answer on Google, you shouldn't be asking the question in an interview or networking meeting. Why should they invest in you if you don't invest first?

Learn to ask well-crafted GLIDE questions. This advanced technique will *significantly* enhance your odds of creating ambassadors and put you ahead of the competition.

A GLIDE Question

→ **G**ets you information that's helpful to your job exploration and is not available online

→ **L**eads to interesting conversation between you and the contact, building the relationship

→ **I**s about something in your contact's knowledge base, which shows you've done your homework

→ **D**emonstrates market or industry knowledge, which shows you've prepared

→ **E**xpresses a skill or expertise you possess that is relevant to the role or company you're targeting

GLIDE helps you prepare questions that uncover the information you are looking for and show *your* value at the same time. Prepare two GLIDE questions for a 15-minute meeting with a contact. This will require research and deep knowledge about yourself, your contact, the company, and the industry, but as someone with a focused Plan A, you already have all this. When you're competing with the clock in an initial meeting to create an ambassador, this strategy will serve you well. Solid GLIDE questions might sound something like these:

Example 1

I noticed on LinkedIn that you're involved with the new product launch in Brazil. That interests me because I spent a year in South America helping my previous company open our LATAM distribution center. Can you tell me more about your role and how the recent legislation has impacted the project?

Example 2

When Maria suggested I reach out to you, she mentioned you also started as a patent attorney before making a transition into product management. What I love about that work is being part of making new ideas come to life. Also, I admittedly enjoy the pressure of tight deadlines and the challenge of coordinating diverse client needs, particularly in technology, which is where I've been specializing in patent work. Can you speak to the core skills you engage from your background as a lawyer in your current role?

These are a great start for creating an ambassador. GLIDE questions lead to interesting conversations, which build rapport, and ultimately, the relationship. While you may truly be interested in the basics about your contact, such as how she got started on this career path or what he enjoys about the company, GLIDE questions enable you to get to this type of information, either in the initial conversation or the next meeting, while also demonstrating *your* motivation, investment, and value.

Impostor Syndrome

Responsibility—Reality—*Risk*—Resilience

AS A SWITCHER, YOU probably thrive on challenges and even seek them out, so you're bound to face times in your career when you feel out of your league. Even fleetingly, as you take on greater responsibility and novel challenges, you may question your competence and ability to succeed in the new situation. "Impostor Syndrome" is characterized by the feeling you are a fraud or somehow not qualified to perform the work you have taken on. It is stressful and creates the irrational fear that someone may find out you don't belong in this role. About 70 percent of people experience impostor syndrome at some point, and high performers who consistently seek out new situations are more susceptible.[4]

The unfortunate result of Impostor Syndrome is that it causes people to undermine their abilities and make excuses for their behavior, which sometimes leads to a self-fulfilling prophecy. Have you ever heard a speaker begin a presentation by saying his flight got in late? Lowering audience expectations is a way to compensate in advance for a potentially poor performance. It also can subconsciously create the *exact* situation you're trying to avoid: You're perceived as less competent. Even worse, Impostor Syndrome can keep you stuck. You become afraid to take risks where you could potentially fail. Have you ever second-guessed your decision to apply for a bigger role because you didn't know if you could pull it off? If so, you're not alone.

Here are seven tips for overcoming Impostor Syndrome:

1. **If you aren't struggling a bit, you aren't growing much.** High achievers know that being the smartest person in the room limits their growth, so they often put themselves into challenging situations intentionally (see Chapter Thirteen for more on this). When you're taking on a new venture like a job switch, it's normal to feel behind the curve. This doesn't mean you're a fraud or not cut out for the work. Don't compare your *start* to someone else's peak.

2. **Quiet that inner voice.** If you were selected for promotion or asked to speak to a group, it's because others recognized your expertise and potential. We're often our own worst critic and hardest on ourselves. If you're new at something, have realistic expectations and give yourself the latitude to learn.

3. **Perfection is slow death.** Perfectionists have an all-or-nothing view. Even as a seasoned expert, you're human and not immune to bad days or learning curves. Mistakes can

indicate that you need to prioritize, delegate, or take a break. Or they could just be mistakes. Don't make them into more than they are.

4. **Honor your accomplishments.** Even with a sea of awards, achievements, or recognitions, it's easy to forget all that when you make a mistake. Life isn't about keeping a scorecard, but don't give more weight to slipups than accomplishments (this is loss aversion rearing its ugly head!). Reminisce about past successes, and then engage strategies that worked before to tackle the problems you're facing.

5. **Drop the "Yes, but . . ."** Do you deflect or write off compliments? Perhaps you attribute your success to luck (external locus of control). We are masters at believing negative feedback while shrugging off the positive. Take time to listen to praise from others and *own* it.

6. **Plan for the worst-case scenario.** The worst-case scenario rarely happens, but if you have an action plan should it become reality, you can be confident you'll handle the lesser obstacles that do arise.

7. **Fake it 'til you make it.** When you come across as self-assured, others sense that and it creates a positive spiral. Self-assurance doesn't mean you have all the answers, rather that you're confident you can use resources to find solutions as problems arise.

Fear can take hold easily when you're approaching unknown situations that are important to you, such as a major career switch. But fear is self-imposed—your brain is trying to protect you from an imagined threat—which means you also have the power to overcome it.

How (Else) to Kick Butt in Networking Meetings

To cover all your bases, here are a few more tips to create an ambassador in your next networking meeting.

☞ **Communicate specifically what you're looking for (your Plan A).** While "being open to anything" may feel like a good approach to increase your options, the exact opposite is true. First, it's inaccurate. Are you *really* willing to work in any location for any pay? Probably not. Second, it leaves too much to chance. Without a target, your contacts may not bring you any information or may filter opportunities based on their (potentially incorrect) assumptions. Either way, fewer leads get back to you.

☞ **Clearly communicate what you're looking for.** This is not the time to use fancy jargon and industry buzzwords. When speaking with your network, use an analogy or example if needed to ensure they have a solid idea of what you're seeking. Many people are too polite or insecure to ask for clarification, so make sure they don't need to. Instead of saying you "initiated the optimization of end-user experience through coding software that minimizes unwanted market disruptions" (huh?), you might say, "You know those annoying pop-up messages on social media? I code the technology that allows you to override them," and then get into more specifics depending on your audience's level of understanding.

☞ **Keep your documents and social media updated.** Ensure your professional social media profile is complete and aligns with your Plan A. The first thing most people will do is look you up online. If your profile is still aligned with the field you're looking to *leave*, it will be confusing. Also, although you shouldn't give your resume out when networking (you're building a relationship, not interviewing for a job . . . yet), have your resume and a cover letter shell prepared. If your contact is aware of an actual job possibility, you don't want to wait a week to send your documents.

☞ **Share specific companies that interest you.** (Note: If the person you're meeting with works for the specific company you're targeting, you can skip this step.) If you tell people you're interested in telecom, specifically Comcast, Verizon, and AT&T, chances are they know someone—a neighbor, cousin, former classmate—who works or has worked in one of those companies. Having a respected employee pass your resume along for an open job can be a huge foot in the door, especially for a Switcher. While most people won't know of a specific job opening, they'll usually know someone who works for a major company.

☞ **Be flexible.** The more restrictions you put on your time, schedule, and ways to connect, the harder you make it for your contacts to meet with you. Be agile and cater to your contacts' schedule. If they tell you they're only available at 7:00 a.m. at the gym, make it work even if you prefer to sleep in. If the only day they're available happens to be on your day off, find a quiet place to take the call. You'll get more meetings if you're flexible. Remember, your contacts are doing *you* a favor.

☞ **Keep the ball in your court.** Everyone's busy, and even friends with the best intentions sometimes get sidetracked. If you don't hear back from a contact after reaching out, try again in two weeks: "I know you're busy, so I wanted to loop back in case you missed my initial email. . . . " If you don't hear back after that, move on because this person likely isn't going to be very helpful anyway. If you drive the process, you'll have much greater success and waste less time. If you wait for the phone to ring or email to come in, you'll likely be waiting a long time. This is not the time to be passive.

IN SUMMARY

You have more power than you think, even as a nontraditional candidate. These job search strategies won't always be comfortable, but they *are* within your control. Further, most traditional candidates likely won't work as hard as you are. This makes you stand out. If you're willing to put in the time, take the risks, and push through the setbacks, a successful career switch is completely within your reach.

CHAPTER NINE SWITCH POINTS

→ Reaching second-level contacts should be a key part of your networking strategy. This is where the action happens, so don't overlook these opportunities.

→ The goal of the initial networking meeting is to get to the second meeting. Networking is a long-term strategy of building relationships.

→ If you're not creating ambassadors, you're not networking effectively. Put in the effort to prepare and do the work for your contacts so they leave impressed and ready to market you to their network.

→ GLIDE questions are the new way to network and will set you apart from other job seekers vying for your contact's attention.

→ Everyone experiences a touch of Impostor Syndrome at one time or another. When it strikes, recall your achievements and know that you're likely on the verge of a professional growth spurt, which is positive.

V

Keep the Ball in Your Court

How to Never Have a Bad Interview

What Are They Really Asking?

It's a much-lamented fact that, in many cases, the most qualified person doesn't get the job—the CEO's nephew does. But as a Switcher, that's good news for you, even if your uncle isn't a CEO. In the hiring game, savvy managers are paying attention to other assets than qualifications, such as recommendations, a collaborative go-getter attitude, a history of achieving profitable results (even if in a different role or industry), the motivation to excel in the position, and the resourcefulness and initiative to learn quickly and solve challenges. As a Switcher, you can highlight these qualities to show the value you'll bring to the role.

The interview is your opportunity to put your experience, skills, and goals together for the hiring team, to paint a clear, cohesive picture of what they are buying. Now's your chance to show how motivated you are and how much work you've already done. In this chapter, you will:

• Learn what you're up against as you compete with traditional candidates in the interview—and how to surge to the top

- Get the inside scoop on the only three things a hiring manager really cares about in an interview and which is most critical for a Switcher
- Learn how to respond to the opening question you'll get in almost every interview to set a positive impression for the rest of the interaction
- Get strategies to handle the toughest interview questions for Switchers
- Learn the one question you absolutely *must* ask at the end of every interview to seal the deal
- Get tips to overcome the obstacles that fear may be creating

Know What You're Up Against— and Make It Work in Your Favor

Getting in front of the decision makers as a Switcher is a big step, so if you've made it this far, congrats! But it's a bit of a false summit, as you still have uphill climbing left to do. You're likely competing with traditional candidates, who still have an advantage over you in the interview process. The hiring manager likely assumes the "traditional" applicant:

- Understands the industry "lingo" and acronyms
- Knows the key players and how to partner with them
- Recognizes what the job is all about
- Can navigate the culture and anticipate the obstacles
- Can hit the ground running without much training

All, some, or none of these assumptions might be true. Regardless, the odds you're facing are tough, but far from impossible. Here are the things that can tip hiring managers in your favor:

- You networked and were referred by someone whose opinion the hirer trusts. (You had a strong endorsement.)

☞ You clearly and concretely articulated how your transferable skills and experience will lead to relevant results in the role. (You effectively rebranded your background.)

☞ You've demonstrated commitment to the career switch by participating in industry events, volunteering for projects to gain skills, and regularly posting content about the field on social media. (You've shown commitment.)

☞ You've kept up with the market in anticipation of the job change and have demonstrated that you can bring practical, fresh ideas and perspectives to the role. (You did your homework.)

☞ Your "career story" is genuine, logical, and supported by actions. (You have a clear plan for how this career fits into your longer-term goals.)

In Chapter Two, I reviewed hirers' hesitations and biases when it comes to hiring Switchers. I showed why, as a Switcher, you cannot cut corners and expect success when interviewing. Thankfully, you've been working through this book, you've navigated the job search well so far, and have already done much of the work that will prepare you for the interview. I'm going to provide you with insights that should look familiar.

The Only Three Things That Matter (and the One Switchers Must Focus On!)

Interviews can be nerve-wracking. Practice and preparation help immensely, but understanding what the person on the other side of the desk is looking for can make all the difference. In my time as a hiring manager and recruiter, I looked for three things in a candidate, and the last of these was the deciding factor *every* time.

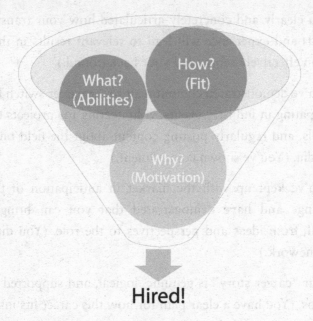

What? (Abilities)

How? (Fit)

Why? (Motivation)

Hired!

Relevant Abilities (the "What")

The need for relevant abilities is a given, and since you've made it to the interview stage, there's a good chance you have the core transferable skills they're looking for. (See Chapter Three for more on ensuring that your skills are aligned with your Plan A.) In a career switch, you can build a solid case by focusing on highly desirable qualities that transcend all roles, such as consistently being a top performer (early promotions, academic honors, employee awards), offering a unique mix of expertise that provides added value to the company (USP), or demonstrating how your transferable skills paired with an ability to learn quickly will enable you to hit the ground running.

All that said, don't rattle off a list of skills in the interview and leave the interviewer to figure out how these skills will contribute to your success in the role. Instead, focus on connecting the dots and showing how your expertise will solve the company's biggest pain points. This requires preparation on your part (which you've likely done to make it this far), and will have a massive impact in the interview.

Fit (the "How")

We've all heard a candidate's fit is critical, but few hiring managers can clearly define what "fit" means to them. It is somewhat arbitrary and relies heavily on the company, team, interviewer, and other complex and uncontrollable factors. Because it's hard to pin down, many hiring managers describe fit as an "I know it when I see it" quality. The result is that candidates similar to the interviewer end up getting an offer because hirers mistake "similar" for "fit."[1] This is a common hiring error.

Interviewers may believe that since *they* personally are successful, hiring someone like themselves makes sense. Worse, untrained hirers unconsciously coach candidates they favor by nodding, smiling, or asking leading questions. The result can be that the candidate *seems* like a great fit, when in fact the hirer biased the interview through subtle feedback. Smart managers know diversity brings fresh ideas, strengths, and energy to a department.

How can you, as a Switcher, prepare to meet a requirement you can't even pin down? First, let's attempt to more concretely define fit, which can be broadly summarized as "how you approach your work and whether or not this matches well with the needs and culture of your company." Fit is the way you make decisions, relate to others, solve problems, lead a team, prioritize, communicate, and perform your work. It can include personality factors such as energy level, and physical style such as your nonverbal actions and appearance.

Noah was attempting an industry transition from banking to a technology startup and continued to get passed over after the initial interview. He typically wore a tailored suit and presented as formal and serious during the conversations. The hirers were wearing flip-flops and T-shirts, while tending to joke around and ask questions about Noah's personal hobbies and interests. Clearly this was a big disconnect, and Noah wasn't perceived as a fit even though his skills were solid enough to land him multiple interviews.

A strong hiring manager looks for someone who can function effectively within the culture and politics of the organization and team to get things accomplished.

Lastly, the search for fit goes both ways. There's no sense trying to be someone you're not just to get an offer, because both you and the team will be miserable after a few months. What you can do in the interview is have a two-way dialogue that also lets you get a sense of the work culture and how it fits you.

Motivation (the "Why")

If the hiring manager has a positive impression of you—the relevant skills and fit seem to be there—the deciding factor will be your motivation. In other words, your answer to the question, "Why do you want this job, in this company, at this time?" will make or break your chances of getting an offer. If abilities and fit are covered, knowing you are motivated to accept the job, work hard at it, and grow with the company over the long term will go a long way to convince the hirer to close the deal. This is where your Career Story comes in.

Because a manager's number one fear is making a hiring mistake, your Career Story as a Switcher needs to make perfect sense to them. Hirers don't care to hear that you're passionate about the role, or that you've always wanted to work at their company. This doesn't differentiate you. They want to know the thought process behind your actions, how you've been preparing for this move, how it fits into your bigger plan, and that you've already taken steps to invest in this path. Your Career Story is like your closing argument at a trial, and the facts are just as important as the emotions they evoke. Refine your Career Story by revisiting Chapter Six.

The Four-Letter "F" Word That's Mucking Up Your Career

Responsibility—Reality—*Risk*—Resilience

FEAR IS ONE OF the few emotions all living beings experience in some form. From an evolutionary point of view, all species need an awareness of danger to survive. For humans, the world does include some legitimate things to fear. However, most of what plagues people cannot be defined as a true threat to our existence. In fact, most things humans fear in modern life are 100 percent *learned*. One of the top phobias in America is the fear of public speaking.[2] Rationally, we know getting on-stage isn't going to kill us. However, as we begin to worry about being judged or making a mistake, our brain interprets this as "danger."

We're not born fearing judgment. After all, if babies worried about being laughed at when falling, they'd never learn to walk. For most things, we *learn* fear. We fear losing what we've earned—our reputation, a relationship, our job. We fear failure. We fear how we'll be judged if we mess up. Fear not only robs us of happiness, but also hampers career success. And, for a Switcher, fear can be a huge obstacle—especially in an interview where you may feel out of your element as a nontraditional candidate.

In the same way we learn fear, we can also *unlearn* it. Here's how:

- **Prepare.** That may be age-old advice, but in a multimedia world that's pulling our attention in a hundred directions, many skimp on this step. It's time to up your game. The more you reduce ambiguity around what's controllable in an interview (planning your outfit, arriving early, researching your audience), the less noise there will be inside your head to create anxiety.

- **Rename fear.** Anxiety and excitement have similar physical effects of increased heart rate and respiration. The difference is that our mind labels anxiety as "negative" and excitement as "positive." So, why not choose another interpretation for the feelings? Instead of worrying about the interview, be excited for the opportunity to share your professional experiences.

- **Stop comparing.** If you look for someone who's better than you, you'll find him. If you look for someone who isn't as good as you, you'll find him, too. Comparing yourself to others may be the top reason people stop pursuing to stretch career goals. Eventually we believe the "I'm not good enough" mantra we subconsciously repeat to ourselves. But you can rework neural connections in your brain to strengthen positive messages by reminding yourself of past successes and challenges you've already overcome.

- **Practice facing fear.** Regularly taking small risks desensitizes you to the fear response. Exposing yourself to novel situations (traveling to a new country) or small public challenges (posting an original blog) causes your body and mind to acclimate to challenges and raises the bar on the level of stress you're able to comfortably handle (in the same way that regular running increases your body's cardio efficiency). In the words of Eleanor Roosevelt, "do one thing each day that scares you."[3] Strengthen that coping muscle!

Forging into unchartered territory after you've attained success in your current profession *is* intimidating. But, you've survived a lot of firsts in your life. Some you even excel at now. A career switch is just another first that will soon become part of your regular life.

Nail the First Question

The first question an interviewer asks is a crucial opportunity to make a memorable first impression and introduce your key messages. In many interviews, hirers open the conversation with some version of "Tell me about yourself." This makes sense: It's a broad question and generally an easy way for your interviewer to get to know you before the "interrogation" begins. You might understandably feel somewhat at a loss as to how to answer such an open-ended question or even think it's just small talk and an insignificant part of the interview. However, first impressions will color the remaining 45 minutes of the interview, and one study showed that interviewers made a determination about hiring the candidate (or not) in the first 90 seconds![4] Don't miss this perfect opportunity to set the tone. Your objective is to sell yourself as the preferred candidate by showing how you solve the company's pain points.

Let's translate this question into what the interviewer is *really* asking: "What are the top two or three qualities, skill sets, or areas of expertise that will enable you to excel in this role and set you apart from other candidates I'll be interviewing?" Now, that's a lot easier to address! Here's how to craft your response.

SWITCH ACTION

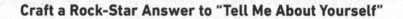

Craft a Rock-Star Answer to "Tell Me About Yourself"

MAKE A GLOWING FIRST impression and set a positive tone for the rest of the interview. Your answer should be:

→ **Relevant.** Focus on what's most important to the interviewer. Your answer should demonstrate your abilities, fit, and motivation to do the job.

→ **Memorable.** Think of your response as a "teaser" for further conversation. Drop in a few tangible achievements you plan to discuss in more detail later in the interview.

→ **Relatable.** Prepare what you want to say, but avoid memorizing a "speech" or sounding overly rehearsed. Your goal in the interview is to *relate* to the hirer. Sounding like a robot will do the opposite and create distance between you.

→ **Concise.** Keep your response to no more than two minutes. This sounds easy, but many unknowingly ramble for four or five minutes. Time yourself when practicing beforehand.

To craft your response to "Tell me about yourself," you can use the format below, pulling from information in your Brand Value Proposition and Career Story. We'll revisit Switcher Greg for an example:

Opening statement. "After 12 successful years in pharma, I'm ready to expand my healthcare expertise and knowledge of technology to focus on product management in the wearable devices industry."

A few career highlights (pick two examples that most relate to your target). "My related strengths include my ability to rally cross-functional teams around a core goal and cut through the red tape associated with doing business overseas, due to my extensive vendor contacts. A few of the projects I'm most proud of are 1) leading a cross-continental team to assess the feasibility of rolling out a new consumer drug in Latin America and then subsequently participating on a successful implementation, and 2) researching the requirements of and implementing a new software program that enabled us to obtain secure legal signatures online, significantly reducing costs and saving time."

Relate your achievements to pain points. "I see these skills being an asset in the product manager role at Scientifica since one of the key goals is overcoming the obstacles of producing and marketing products outside of the U.S., and my experience and contacts will give me an edge in expediting the process. Also, my knack for quickly getting up to speed with technology and being able to communicate user requirements across multiple levels and functions seems to be core to the needs of the role."

Include your Unique Selling Point. "An added bonus is that my prior experience as an attorney gives me the knowledge to understand and deconstruct complicated legislation that could otherwise hold up a project."

Close with why you're excited about this role. "In addition to being a strong match for my strengths in healthcare and technology, what most attracted me to this position is the focus on diabetes prevention, for which there is a rapidly growing need worldwide. I'm confident I can apply my skills and knowledge to make a difference by helping your company to expand your products into a global landscape."

Now it's time to try this by writing your response in your journal. Imagine this is the *only* question you get to answer in the entire interview. To make your best impression, what would you be certain to include while covering the main points and staying under two minutes?

A less common variation on this opening question is, "Walk me through your resume [or background]." As a Switcher you might hear it in interviews, so it's best to prepare for it. With this request, interviewers are looking for a chronological response featuring key career decision points, related accomplishments, and strong transitions. Start with your earlier experiences and describe how you got where you are now. Here are tips for doing this as a nontraditional candidate.

- Include the information from your Brand Value Proposition and Career Story arranged chronologically in alignment with your career history.

- Focus on accomplishments and experiences that directly relate to your target. These can include relevant unpaid roles and part-time gigs.
- Skip the play-by-play rundown of titles, education, and dates, which is dry, but also less relevant as a Switcher. You can pick and choose the most impactful details to highlight.
- Be human and conversational—your main goal is to connect with the interviewer and tee up the rest of the conversation.
- Use impressive transitions such as, "After that project, I was promoted to lead engineer . . .".

If past job titles or experiences detract from your new brand, simply leave them out. Greg might say, "After being recruited by BioTech, Inc. to lead the negotiations of new contracts with our domestic suppliers, I was quickly promoted to oversee this process globally, which exposed me to a host of vendors and customers overseas." Convey relevant information without dwelling on titles that don't align with your new brand, like "lawyer" in Greg's case.

You've likely noticed by now that the time you put into formulating your Plan A, identifying your Brand Value Proposition, and crafting your Career Story has been well spent. You'll use this information throughout the entire job search process (e.g., resume, cover letter, social media, networking, interviews) to demonstrate that your career switch is well thought out and to generate confidence that you're the person for the job!

Tackle the Toughest Interview Questions for the Switcher

A hiring manager's *primary* job function is not interviewing or hiring employees (unless he works in HR). So interview skills are not a core expertise, and there are an array of interviewing styles and questioning techniques. They can range from the "la-di-da" (random conversation) style to the "trickster" (invalid gimmicks) method with several variations in between. The executive assessment firm ghSMART calls this disorderly approach to acquiring talent "voodoo hiring," and, on occasion, the interview process can be as wacky as the name implies.[5]

Many hirers don't have extensive training in interviewing so they may not truly know whether their questions are valid or will get them the information they need for an informed decision.

By the time you get to the interview, you've most likely passed the "basic qualifications" test, so at this point most hiring managers want to know the same general things: Will you be effective in this job (i.e., not require a lot of hand-holding), a good fit with the team (i.e., easy to work with), and motivated to stay (i.e., you're committed)? They will also be keen to pick up on any red flags, and as a Switcher, your nontraditional background will likely be a topic of focus.

When you go into the interview knowing there is no set formula for the interviewer to follow and prepared with what information you want to be certain to convey, you leave less up to chance. So, for every question in the interview, consider "What are they really asking?" ("WATRA"), and then decide which of your relevant achievements you want to use to answer the question. Below are a few common interview questions for Switchers and recommendations for how to respond.

QUESTION: Why Are You Interested in This Job/ Company?

WATRA: How do I know this isn't an impulsive career change? I need to understand how this fits into your overall career path and that this isn't just a fluke or running from a bad employment situation.

Your Response: Share your Career Story.

QUESTION: Why Should I Hire You (Over the Other Qualified Candidates)?

WATRA: How can I be sure you'll work out? This is a risk for me. Ease my mind that hiring you would be a smart decision and that I won't have to put in a lot of extra time training you.

Your Response: Convey your Brand Value Proposition (BVP), and then discuss how your USP (Unique Selling Point) will add extra benefit to the company. Include a specific example of where you've been successful in a new or ambiguous situation with little guidance.

QUESTION: Have You Ever Done [X Task or Y Skill]?

WATRA: This job requires a specific skill set. I'm pretty sure based on your nontraditional background you haven't done this, but I want to hear specifically how you'll be resourceful and overcome this deficiency.

Your Response: Before diving in with "No, I haven't . . ." answer the question he or she is really asking. For example, "I know the Cybextra program is a core software used by your sales team, and although I don't have direct experience with that system, in my last two roles I was required to learn company-specific technology to be effective in my position, and was able to be self-sufficient on the tools within a week of starting. Technology is a lifelong interest of mine, so I enjoy learning new systems and pick them up very quickly."

QUESTION: How Will You Motivate Your Team to Meet Your Goals?

WATRA: How will you garner respect from the team and our clients without a traditional background? How you perform in front of my peers and customers reflects on me. Convince me you won't make me look bad and reassure me you'll quickly get up to speed and earn the respect of others.

Your Response: Read between the lines to answer the *right* question. Demonstrate your leadership skills through examples ("In my last management position, three of my five direct reports were promoted to higher roles . . .") while also acknowledging that you won't have all of the answers but have a plan and smarts to figure it out ("Having managed several project teams in my career, I've had to quickly learn each member's strengths to mobilize the group to effectively execute on the deliverable . . .").

Ace Behavioral Questions with SOART Stories

Behavioral questions typically sound like, "Tell me about a time . . ." or "Describe a situation when. . .". They're common ways to uncover specific skill sets relevant to the job, with the premise that past behavior is predictive of future behavior. So it's important to know that the interviewer is looking for concrete examples that demonstrate *competencies,* which are categories of transferable skills, knowledge, and abilities. As a Switcher, you may not have direct experience, but you've certainly completed projects or assignments that share the same competencies.

The question "Tell me about a difficult client you worked with and how you handled it" gets at your ability to effectively engage the competencies of customer service, negotiation, and possibly conflict management or creative problem-solving. If you haven't worked with external clients in previous roles, think about your internal customers.

The winning approach to answering these questions is easy to remember and use. SOART stories follow this progression:

Situation - Briefly describe the context and key players in your example to set the scene.

Obstacle - Few projects go off without a hitch, so include any challenges you overcame to succeed. This makes your response more credible and your result more powerful.

Action - Describe what specific actions you took to achieve the outcome. These should demonstrate your ability to effectively perform the competencies in question.

Result - Hiring Managers know that the results you've achieved in previous positions (e.g., increasing profits, reducing turnover, etc.) are also outcomes you are likely to produce at their company.

Takeaway - Show how you've grown professionally from the experience. Briefly discuss what you've learned and how it makes you a stronger candidate for this role.

When choosing your SOART stories, dig into the question and think about what competencies the hirer wants to hear about. If the hirer asks about a successful management experience, but you've never had direct reports, recognize that the key skills the hirer is looking for likely include motivating others, displaying decisiveness, coaching or providing feedback, and managing performance. If you've led a project team or have been responsible for delegating tasks to others, you likely have a SOART story that will work to demonstrate your competence in this area.

Pick one example that best demonstrates what the hirer is looking for. Choosing recent examples (within the last two to three years) is preferable, but it's most important to select a story that showcases the requested competency. Here is an example:

Interviewer: "Tell me about a time when you had to fix a major problem for a client." (Competencies: Agility, Resourcefulness, Creativity, Problem-solving.)

Your Response: "When planning the annual conference where we bring in over three hundred team members for a full week from offices across two continents, our usual venue was suddenly unavailable due to a major renovation project resulting from a kitchen fire *(Situation)*. In addition, our budget for the conference was cut by 10 percent *(Obstacle)*. I immediately got on the phone with my contacts and started researching new local venues *(Action)* since many of the attendees had already booked their flights *(More Obstacles)*.

After several conversations, I found another venue that could accommodate the size of our group, but it was more expensive than our regular location *(More Obstacles)*. So I got creative with the menus to get the price lowered *(Action)*. I also negotiated with our original venue to get a 25 percent discount next year with a guaranteed booking, since we were inconvenienced this year *(Actions)*. They agreed, and the reduced cost of the conference over two years actually saved us money *(Result)*.

What I learned from this situation is that limited resources can inspire creativity and that keeping my relationships with vendors strong is worth it, which is something that's also important in the account executive role in your new territory *(Takeaway)*."

SWITCH ACTION

Punch Line First!

USING SOART STORIES IS also a helpful way to create accomplishment-based bullet points for your resume. Look at what competencies your stories are highlighting, then make sure those competencies are clearly demonstrated in bullets on your resume. Here's the cool part for Switchers: Depending on what information in a story you *emphasize* (the "punch line"), you can alter the example to align with a variety of career paths. This allows a Switcher to show how previous experience matches the needs of the new target job. From the previous example SOART story, here are a few variations:

Competencies: Negotiation, Creativity, Organization

- *Saved costs by negotiating a creative* two-year strategy including a 25 percent discount with key vendors, while organizing the annual company conference for over 300 team members

Competencies: Customer Service, Coordination, and Planning

- *Recognized for stellar customer service by skillfully organizing* the annual company conference for over 300 global employees on a 10 percent reduced budget, delivering a high-quality experience for participants

Competencies: Adaptability, Problem-Solving, Calm Under Pressure

- *Demonstrated excellent agility in quickly reorganizing* a 300-person, weeklong global conference after the booked venue unexpectedly canceled the reservation, resulting in a seamless experience for attendees and a negotiated cost-savings of 25 percent over two years.

Competencies are generally transferable, so as a Switcher you likely have some related experience you can describe. In fact, the adapted resume bullet points in the text box show how you can use the same example to demonstrate multiple competencies. Just be careful not to use the same *story* over and over to answer multiple interview questions. Prepare several SOART stories to choose from.

Job Search TMI

You are marketing your value to potential employers. While it's never acceptable to lie about a qualification, you also don't need to share every career misstep or relay your biggest faults. Avoid bringing up the following during interviews, which are all too much information (TMI):

- **The fact that you're a Switcher.** Okay, you're a nontraditional candidate; they get it. Avoid reminding the hirer by using phrases like "Although I'm new to this field . . ." or "I've never done . . ." or "I've always wanted to try . . ." Don't talk about "making a change" or "switching careers." Instead use phrases like "broadening my impact" or "expanding my career to the next level." The more you can normalize the shift, the less the hirer will focus on the risk.

- **Your greatest weakness.** Most interviewers ask you to tell them about a weakness or failure, but there's no need to share when, in your first job, you caused your employer to lose its largest client. That was unfortunate, but I'm sure you've learned a great deal since then. Find an example that shows you're human, but doesn't cause alarm. Stick to skills, not personality traits because they're difficult to change. As a Switcher, you might be tempted to talk about your nontraditional background. Don't. Pick a software program or some other skill that can be easily learned and that any candidate—traditional or not—might be working to improve.

- **Too much personal stuff.** Even if you're hitting it off famously with the recruiter, until you show up for orientation (and likely for 90 days afterward), you're still being evaluated. If you share details about your Vegas trip, hirers will factor that in negatively when making decisions. Recruiters are trained to make you feel comfortable, but remain professional at all times. A candidate once shared her divorce troubles with me, and as you can guess, this didn't make her a front-runner.

Your Last Question Is the Game Changer

Asking insightful questions in an interview allows you to learn more about the role, convey interest in the job, and demonstrate savvy about the company. But truly, asking questions makes or breaks the interview. Once you've prepared for all their tough questions, take more time to consider what *you* will ask when the hirer turns things over to you. An interview is a two-way dialogue, so get the data, facts, and information you need to understand if this job is right for you.

You can use the GLIDE technique (see Chapter Nine) as one strategy for developing your interview questions. The formula will help create insightful questions that inspire meaningful dialogue while also obtaining information you need. Here's one:

In my initial phone meeting with Diane in the Recruiting Department, I learned one of the team's key priorities this year is to centralize all distribution centers into four main regions across the U.S. Having experienced a similar situation earlier in my career when I managed the consolidation of two manufacturing plants, I understand the cost benefits, but also know this type of restructuring can have an impact on jobs. How do you see this change affecting your operations team, and specifically the role I'm applying to?

There are several helpful books on interviewing, so I won't get into too much more detail here. However, there is one Key Question you should ask at the end of *every* interview, especially as a Switcher:

"Is there anything about my background or experience that concerns you about my ability to be successful in this job?"

There are a few good reasons why you need to ask this key question.

Keep the Ball in Your Court

Because many hiring managers have limited training in conducting an interview, regardless of the questions asked it is *your* responsibility to clearly communicate your core qualifications. If the interviewer fails to inquire about leadership experience, she may later assume you don't have the skill set to be a manager. It happens more than you might think. I had a client who was a Certified Professional Accountant, which was indicated on his resume but didn't come up in the interview. He wasn't hired because . . . wait for it . . . he didn't have a core qualification for the role . . . a CPA! The key question can prompt interviewers to ensure they have the data they need for an informed decision.

Avoid Interviewer Bias and Assumptions

Interviewers are human. Humans make assumptions, and many go unexamined, as we covered in Chapter Two. The key question allows you to erase doubt the interviewer may have about hiring you. She may respond, "I'm concerned this will be a very long commute for you." You can then eliminate this concern: "My sister and her family live near this area, so I'm here frequently and look forward to visiting them more often."

Address the Hirer's Concerns

If the hiring manager has no concerns, the key question forces him to "psychologically close" on you as a good match. Consider the response, "Well, no. I can't really think of any concerns." This won't guarantee an offer, but it encourages the hirer to reach a positive conclusion about your candidacy. This can have huge benefits.

While you can ask the key question in a way most comfortable for you, avoid asking "Am I a good fit for the role?" Although it seems like a similar question, this wording puts hirers on the spot and limits how they can respond. You may get an awkward "um, yes," but making your interviewer uncomfortable isn't a positive way to start a long-term relationship.

If the interviewer expresses vague concerns, ask her to be more specific to ensure you address the *right* concern. Say the hirer responds, "I'm concerned the vice president might be intimidated by you," don't automatically spout your ability to get along with everyone. This likely won't assuage her fears. Instead, think about what the hirer is really asking. Try this: "Thank you for your candor. I can see why a good relationship with the vice president is critical for success in the role. Can you be more specific about what might be intimidating, so I have the opportunity to address it?" This strategy helps you avoid a trite response, reassures the recruiter you recognize the concern as valid, and solicits information to adequately address the issue. While this won't lead to an automatic offer, *not* addressing a hiring manager's concern can lead to a rejection.

IN SUMMARY

Throughout this book, your goal has been to get the interview. It's the final stretch in the race between you and a handful of competitors. The most important takeaway from this chapter is that you can't count on a hirer to ask the "right" questions or give you openings to discuss what's most relevant and impressive. Determine specifically what information you want to leave on the table in the interview. The onus is on you.

CHAPTER TEN SWITCH POINTS

→ The three things that matter to an interviewer are abilities, fit, and motivation, the last of which is what will ultimately convince a hirer to pull the trigger and make an offer.

→ Be prepared to start your interview with a compelling answer to the frequently asked question, "Tell me about yourself."

→ Get into the mind of the interviewer and strive to understand the WATRA behind each question so you can relay the most relevant information and examples.

→ Rehearse potentially awkward situations to get more comfortable and avoid TMI.

→ Use SOART stories to answer behavioral-based interview questions in a structured and concise manner. Shifting the punch line can help you highlight different competencies.

→ Close strong with insightful questions, including the key question, which will wipe concerns off the table and secure you as a viable candidate.

→ Fear is a learned response—tackle it head-on so it doesn't become an obstacle in your Switch.

It's Not Fair

(It Really Isn't!)

Uttered by third graders and politicians alike, "It's not fair" is a phrase we hear a lot. To me, the phrase is the equivalent of "the earth is round" or "the sky is blue"—it's a well-known reality that life, indeed, is not fair. Part of the problem is that definitions of fairness vary. For some, fairness means sameness (everyone gets an equal-sized slice of pizza). For others, fairness means justice (an eye for an eye) or getting what you deserve (I work hard, so I should be rewarded). No matter how you define it, fairness is in the eye of the beholder. The sooner you accept that, the better off you are.

By now, you've likely experienced rejection or disappointment in your job search. It's an inevitable part of a transition, and Switchers must endure more than most job seekers. The toughest part of a career switch is the mental stamina it takes to remain positive, motivated, and focused during this process. In this chapter, we'll take a break from the tools and mechanics of the job search to focus on strategies for defeating the curveballs and frustrations you're likely experiencing by this point. In this chapter, you will learn:

- Why you're better served by accepting the unfair reality and working within those bounds
- How to cope with rejection in networking and interviews
- How to handle rude recruiting practices
- Why it's a bad idea to cease job search efforts when you're about to get an offer
- How to keep the ball in your court throughout the job search process
- How changing your perspective can help your switch

Accept What Is, Not What Should Be

In the job search, making the mistake of chasing fairness leads to frustration and disappointment. Job seekers desperately want the hiring process to be logical, sequential, and concrete, when it's more often irrational, circular, and abstract. And, unfortunately, very unfair.

- It's not fair your coworker got the promotion even though you have more experience.
- It's not fair they hired a younger applicant for the role.
- It's not fair you were laid off and the new person wasn't.
- It's not fair you were the most qualified candidate, yet the CEO's nephew got the job.
- It's not fair they won't take a chance on you as a Switcher.

Let's face it, when as a Switcher you get hired into a role you aren't exactly the most qualified for, all those traditional applicants you beat out will think *that's* not fair.

It's not fair, but it *is* reality. This is a hard pill to swallow because it threatens our sense of control. To accept that life isn't fair, we must acknowledge there are no guarantees or absolutes, which is unsettling (see Chapter Two for more on why this is so hard). You have two choices: chase the illusion of fairness (a no-win game), or accept circumstances as they are and figure out how to get what you want *within the realm of reality*.

Bestselling author Debbie Ford wisely pointed out that instead of taking ownership for our circumstances, many of us go to our "graves blaming others for the condition of our lives"—and that resentment is the very obstacle that keeps us stuck in unhappiness and dissatisfaction.[1] Whether or not you agree with the situation is another story for another book. Because to reach your goals, you'll be more successful putting energy into chasing *results* instead of chasing fairness. In this chapter, we'll look at the "unfair" situations Switchers commonly face, and talk about how to deal with them.

My Networking's Not Working!

Many job seekers deny the power of networking in favor of less effective strategies. I used to be one of them until I relented to the research and decided to make it a way of life: That's when magic started happening. Successful Switchers know networking is integral, so they give it all they've got. If you feel you've put your heart and soul into networking, but aren't seeing the results you want, don't lament that you're doomed. Instead, take a moment to first evaluate these possibilities:

👉 **Is your message muddled or inconsistent?** Are you being clear about your Plan A, or is the message getting lost in translation? People will hesitate to recommend you to their contacts if your career switch seems impulsive or if they aren't sure what you're specifically seeking. Check with an objective friend to ensure your message is consistent, has conviction, and makes sense to others—especially people with a different professional background.

☞ **Are you taking a "one and done" approach?** If you're not looping back with contacts or investing in relationships, they're likely not advocating on your behalf. To reap the rewards, you need to create ambassadors through repeated contact over time. So take an honest look at your follow-through (see Chapter Nine for ideas).

☞ **Did you wait until you needed something?** Networking is about planting seeds, so it will take a little time before you start reaping what you've sown. Make networking a regular part of your life so the benefits are constant. Make it a habit even when you're not in a job search.

☞ **Are you overlooking the power of second-level contacts?** Everyone you meet has something to offer. Whether that's insight, information, or connections to others, each person can teach you something. You never know who may be connected to the manager of the team you want to be on or the human resources director of the company you want to join. Don't underestimate people; they can surprise you.

☞ **Are you neglecting to create ambassadors?** Meeting new people is great but, if you're not creating the ambassadors I talked about in Chapter Nine, then you're only adding names to your list. Ambassadors will spread your expertise to others, bring you helpful information, and be advocates for you when they come across an opportunity.

If you can honestly answer "no" to all the questions above, chances are your networking *is* working, but perhaps not as quickly or as directly as you'd like. Not every contact will lead to something tangible right away, and if that's your expectation, you'll be disappointed. (One of my networking activities led to a job offer *seven years later!*) If you're feeling frustrated, that's completely normal—you're climbing a rugged mountain—but don't let that frustration become another obstacle. Take a break, regroup, get input from a friend or a career coach, and then carry on.

Rude Recruiting

Perhaps even worse than rejection is being ghosted. UrbanDictionary.com defines "ghosting" as suddenly ceasing all communications with someone after establishing an initial relationship. There's no explanation, and you're left wondering what the heck happened. In the hiring process, applicants can be ghosted at any time, from the phone screen through the third interview! A candidate believes things are going well, only to never hear from the recruiter again.

You already know the process can be discouraging. While you can't control a company's hiring practices or responsiveness, there are things you can do:

☞ **Assess.** First, determine if you're truly being ghosted. Hiring happens at a glacial pace. Managers have a primary job, and it isn't hiring. Even if it's on their to-do list, it likely isn't at the very top, especially when business demands are high. Two or even three weeks can easily pass before replying to you.

☞ **Plan.** Before ending the interview, ensure you have the hirer's contact information so you can follow up. Ask when you can expect to hear about next steps and politely let the hirer know if you haven't heard by then, you'll call a day or two later. Gaining permission to follow up makes picking up the phone easier when the time comes. The hirer also recognizes you'll be anticipating a reply, so you're less likely to be ghosted.

☞ **Act.** At the two-week mark, if you haven't heard anything, send a brief email reiterating your interest in the role and inquiring about next steps. If another seven to ten days pass, try once more. If you're waiting on a response from a recruiter, try reaching out directly to the hiring manager instead. While they probably aren't interested in hiring you since nearly a month has passed without contact, making an effort to close the process on a gracious note is wise. It's quite possible the company liked you and would consider you for a future opening (if *you're* still interested at this point, that is).

☞ **Strategize.** Engage your network. Candidates who network into a company are typically treated better. If you aren't getting a response, check with your network to see if you can get insider information. Perhaps the position was filled internally, there's a hiring freeze, or the project you were applying for has been postponed. It's better to know than to keep wondering. Insider contacts make the hiring process much less of a mystery.

Use the information you gathered during the hiring process. If the process is disorganized and the company representatives fail to treat applicants with basic respect, this might be a glimpse into how the company functions overall. It's worth probing to find out if it's just a rogue hirer or a more pervasive issue. You may avoid a possible disaster.

Being ghosted by a company feels personal, but it isn't. Recognize it's a negative reflection on the company, not you. The best thing you can do in a job search is to pursue multiple roles with a variety of employers simultaneously so you don't get hung up waiting on one. Too many factors beyond your control can halt the process, like a change in strategy or budget cuts. The more balls you have in the air, the less frustrated you'll get if you're ghosted.

Rejection Happens

One of the most difficult things to hear after a job interview is, "You didn't get the position." Rejection is disappointing no matter what the situation. Humans have a natural need to feel like we belong and are accepted. However, some things in life are fraught with rejection, and the job search is one of them, especially for a Switcher. In an online poll by Careerealism.com, 28 percent of respondents indicated they sent out around 50 applications for every interview they landed, and about 33 percent reported they sent out about 10 applications for every interview.[2] While it's hard to generalize because of the differences across roles, industries, and other factors, what's clear is that rejection is common in job searches.

It can feel even worse after what felt like a great interview. By this stage, you may be planning your daily commute, thinking about how it will feel to work with the team, and even visualizing what your business cards will say. You're starting to get emotionally invested. It's enough to make anyone giddy, which only makes news that another candidate was selected more crushing. Here are some tips to make the blow of rejection a little easier to take:

- ☞ **Recognize rejection goes both ways.** According to Forbes, in 2012, 56 percent of all employers reported that a candidate rejected their job offer in the last year.[3] After all, you can only accept one job and employers can only hire one candidate.

- ☞ **Have a realistic mindset.** If you go in estimating that one in every ten applications will lead to an interview, and one in five interviews will lead to a second interview, you won't be as frustrated when you get a few "Thanks, but no thanks" emails. Note: getting a referral significantly increases these odds.

- ☞ **Put rejection into perspective.** The company decided you were not the best candidate for this job right now. That's it. Don't make it about your overall worth or talent. Dust off, and move forward.

☞ **Define rejection appropriately.** Candidates can be extremely disappointed about not getting offered a job they *knew* wasn't a good fit anyway. What looked perfect on paper turned out to be a poor match during the interview process. The company likely realized this, too. This is a win-win: It saves you both from wasting time on a bad match.

As Jia Jiang reminds us in *Rejection Proof*, rejection "is just an opinion."[4] For some, it gets easier with time. For others, rejection continues to sting. Unless you're sitting at home doing nothing, you're going to experience rejection. In fact, the more novel things you try, the more you will fail, be rejected, and make mistakes—but proportionally, the more awesome things you will learn and achieve as well.

The Middle Seat

Responsibility—Reality—Risk—*Resilience*

ANYONE WHO TRAVELS ON airlines knows the many hassles associated with getting from point A to point B. Case in point: the dreaded middle seat. When you set up a customer profile for an airline, most ask your seating preference, offering the choice of "window" or "aisle." I've yet to be asked if I prefer the "middle." This makes sense. Most people value personal space, and although the aisle and window seats are not more spacious, we are psychologically uncomfortable being sandwiched between two strangers for several hours.

However, like most things in life, this depends on context and perspective. Consider this: You're rushing to fly home to be back in time for your second grader's debut as Turkey #4 in the Thanksgiving play. Or you're trying to catch the last flight out to make an important client meeting the next morning. In these situations, you might be happy to fly in the overhead compartment just to secure a spot. The middle seat transforms from a nightmare into a thing of beauty.

Life is all about perspective. Any situation can look better or worse depending on the context and our view of the circumstances. Although we don't always have control over the context, we *do* have the freedom to determine our attitude. As a Switcher, this will keep you sane. Next time you find yourself in the proverbial middle seat, why not change your perspective, sit back, and enjoy the journey? That choice is always yours.

Don't Stop 'Til You're There

Runner Ben Payne was near the finish line of a 10k race, holding his victory finger proudly in the air. As Ben was about to hit the tape, Scott Overall passed him and won the race by 9/100s of a second! Ben hit cruise-control too early and lost the gold. It was an unfortunate mistake, and job seekers are not immune to it.

Think about it. You had a fantastic first interview and just got called to schedule the second! The job seems like a phenomenal match and you're anticipating your first day. Your job search has been frustrating, marked by dead end after dead end, but you can feel it: *this is the one!* What should you do next? Keep searching.

This is the opposite of what most job seekers do. Once a "perfect" opportunity gains momentum, they slow down or stop other search activities, rationalizing it doesn't make sense to pester their network or start a new application. While it's commendable to be optimistic, it's also wise to keep searching. Until you have an official offer in hand, you're still in the race and it's anyone's game.

Remember: Life isn't fair and it pays to be prepared for anything. While you're daydreaming about your office, a strong internal candidate may apply for the job. The company may move the job to their Chicago branch. The salary offered may be below what you can accept. And on and on. There are no guarantees, so keep searching until you sign on the dotted line.

The worst-case scenario if you keep searching *and* get the dream job? You may have two good offers, get to choose the best match, and have leverage to negotiate a higher salary.

Keep the Ball in Your Court

My best advice for Switchers is to *always keep the ball in your court*. After all, you're the one with the goal, so be persistent and assertive to keep driving the process forward. It may not be fair that you were ghosted after an awesome interview or networking meeting. But don't wallow in defeat. Act! Here are strategies for constantly keeping the ball in your court:

- **When writing a cover letter.** Close the letter in a respectfully assertive manner, letting the reader know you'll follow up. "I will contact you next week to answer any questions you might have about the materials I have submitted." Then find a way to get the contact information and reach out.

- **When emailing a networking contact.** Asking contacts for their time can be intimidating. People are busy, so the more clarity you provide, the more you increase your odds of getting a positive response. Be specific about what you want, and let the contact know you'll limit the call to 15 minutes (lunch or coffee can take too much time). End your request with, "I know you're extremely busy. If I don't hear from you, I'll follow up at the end of next week to check in."

- **When reconnecting with a networking contact.** In my experience, giving your resume to a new contact when there isn't a specific opening in the company is the kiss of death. People tend to ask for your resume so they can "pass it along" as a passive way of indicating they don't plan on doing much to help you. Steve Dalton calls these contacts "Obligates" as opposed to Boosters.[5] Someone who doesn't want to help probably won't, but try once more before handing over your resume by saying, "Thanks, Art. It's very generous of you to offer to send my resume to your contacts. While I may take you up on that soon, right now what would be most helpful is an introduction to the head of finance in your company." Based on your contact's response, you'll be able to tell if he is an Obligate or Booster, and then proceed accordingly.

☞ **When following up with a contact.** Your goal in a networking meeting is to create an ambassador. This may take a few meetings or follow-ups to cultivate the relationship. Create a follow-up loop at the end of each conversation. "Alicia, I really appreciated your time today. Can I reach out next month to see how things turned out with the budget planning? I'm really interested in Caltex and would love to be considered if the team decides to add head count." Here's another scenario. Perhaps you ask your contact for an introduction to someone in the legal department. Maybe she hedges. That's fine—she may not have a name on the spot or she may be looking for a graceful exit. To find out, keep the ball in your court! Respond, "That would be great, Cyndy. I know you're busy, so I'll check in with you again at the end of the month." This may feel assertive if you're not used to holding people to their word. But you'll know at the end of the month if Cyndy will come through. Then you can use your time wisely and not waste it on contacts who aren't interested in helping further.

☞ **When closing the interview.** Before exiting, ask about next steps in the hiring process. Hiring managers will often say you'll "hear something in the next week or two." Keep the ball in your court! Respond with, "That sounds great, Cathy. I'm very interested in this role and look forward to next steps. If I don't hear from you by next Friday, I'll give you a call to check in."

Keeping the ball in your court takes courage, but you'll be glad you did. It beats the waiting game, agonizing over whether your email address got lost or if the position was filled with another candidate. Limbo is the *worst*! Further, driving the process shows you're confident, motivated, and interested—the exact qualities that employers value.

SWITCH ACTION

Keep the Ball in Your Court

ONE WAY TO MAKE keeping the ball in your court easier is to use language that is comfortable for you. Don't soften the message; rather, choose words that feel authentic to your style and personality. Regardless of the situation, an assertive close will give you a small sense of control over this traditionally ambiguous process. Craft your own "Keep the ball in your court" statements and practice using them until they feel like second nature. Come up with statements to use in various situations. If you're still struggling with this step, look at it this way: Everyone is juggling a dozen demands. Knowing that *you'll* follow up if they forget does your contacts a favor—it means they can't drop this ball.

IN SUMMARY

Your job search will present many obstacles to overcome—unfair practices, rude recruiting, rejection. None of these is unusual, so don't stall your search by taking them personally. Anticipating and strategizing for obstacles is critical to overcoming them. Maintain a positive outlook, evaluate your tactics, and course correct where needed, but keep moving forward, with the ball firmly in your court.

CHAPTER ELEVEN SWITCH POINTS

→ The job search is unfair. That's true, but don't complain about it; instead, use it to your advantage as a Switcher.

→ Hirers are not always responsive. It can be frustrating, but it's not personal. Be gracious and persistent to get the information you need to keep moving your job search forward.

→ Keep putting 100 percent into your job search until you've signed on the dotted line. Unexpected obstacles can arise so don't make the mistake of slowing down the search.

→ Keep the ball in your court. Some things are beyond your control in a career switch, so take a lead role on those things you *can* control.

→ Embrace the "middle seat." Your attitude can have a big impact in the job search, so choose a positive one.

Always Sleep on It

Get Ready to Negotiate!

You have probably accepted at least a few job offers by this point in your career, but how often have you negotiated for a higher salary before taking the job? If your answer is "not often" or "never," you're not alone. Negotiating is tricky, and how much difference can that extra few thousand dollars make, anyway? The answer is, a hefty difference. According to one study, assuming an average annual pay increase of 5 percent, an employee whose starting yearly salary was $55,000 rather than $50,000 would earn an additional $600,000 or more over the course of a 40-year career.[1] So clearly, it's worth negotiating, every time—even when you're switching careers.

This chapter has loads of information about how to negotiate a job offer as a Switcher, but usually the biggest barrier isn't "how," it's mustering the courage to do it. We can come up with seemingly rational reasons why it doesn't make sense to negotiate. But as a hirer, when a candidate didn't negotiate after I extended the offer, my first thought was, "I made a hiring mistake." Talking about money can feel awkward, especially for Switchers, so in this chapter I'll share tips from my experience negotiating on both sides of the desk. As you read, you will learn:

- Why it's important to always negotiate, even if you're happy with the initial offer
- How to engage psychology principles to negotiate a better compensation package
- How to negotiate professionally and effectively to deepen your relationship with your new boss
- Why sometimes, as a Switcher, you'll need to take a pay cut, at least temporarily
- What to do when you have two good offers on the table
- How failure is a critical step to success

If You Don't Ask, You Don't Get

About four months after starting one of my first corporate jobs out of college, I realized my colleagues in similar roles had received a sign-on bonus, but I hadn't. Why not? The answer is simple: I didn't ask for one and they did. From then on, I vowed to always negotiate job offers.

If you don't ask for what you want, the answer is always "no." I could end this section with that statement—however, there are other compelling reasons to negotiate a job offer. When I ask people why they settled for the initial offer, they tell me, "I was afraid they would renege on the offer," or "I was pretty happy with the first offer." In my many years of coaching, I've never heard of a case where an offer was taken off the table because someone politely asked for flexibility. And, even if the initial offer is more than you expected, would you (or your partner or kids) be *less* happy if you earned 10 percent more each month or had an extra week of vacation? No way!

After a long search, it's understandable why you might say yes to the initial offer and be done with it, especially if it's decent. But take a night to sleep on it and discuss it with a spouse or friend, because no job seeker can weigh all the possibilities in the moment, especially when emotions are high with the fantastic news. Diane, a double-Switcher who was offered a role, almost blurted out "Yes!" after her exhausting search. But she caught herself and asked for a day to review the offer with her family. She negotiated additional vacation days, and was glad she remembered this advice! Discussing money can be uncomfortable. But isn't 10 minutes of discomfort worth several thousand dollars?

Beyond the financial gain, there are other advantages to negotiating. The salary discussion is your first opportunity to have a real conversation with your new boss. In the job, you'll need his or her support in a variety of work situations. The salary negotiation is an early chance to see if your new manager will advocate for you, which is good to know up front. Negotiating likely will not distance you. It can do the opposite: Having a difficult discussion and finding a mutual solution *deepens* the relationship. Also, in some fields, like sales, it can be detrimental *not* to negotiate. After all, negotiating and influencing are key skills in your new role, so if you skip them the hiring manager may be concerned.

As a Switcher, you may feel you're not entitled to ask for more money. After all, you were lucky just to get the offer, right? Wrong. If you were offered the job, the company recognizes the value you bring and they want you to start the job excited and motivated. You may also be questioning your ability to perform the role as well as a traditional candidate. Don't. While things may feel ambiguous now, six months into the job you'll no doubt be fully up to speed and wondering why you were worried in the first place. Remember, all future raises, bonuses, and merit increases will be calculated as a percentage of your starting salary. It's much harder to get a large bump in base pay once you are inside.

I'll let you in on a little secret: Once a company makes an offer, *they* are in the hot seat, worrying you might not accept. The hiring manager has likely endured a long search as well, and wants this process to be over as much as you do. The hirer is already envisioning you on the team getting work done. So, you have a little leverage at this point. The tables have finally turned.

Negotiations don't need to focus only on your paycheck. While you want to get your base pay as high as possible as a first step, many other aspects of a compensation package can be negotiated: extra vacation time, relocation dollars, a sign-on bonus, virtual work days, tuition reimbursement, parking costs, start date, association dues—the list goes on. Think about what is most meaningful to you or what would leave you with more money in your pocket at the end of each month. My friend Maria's company agreed to pay her cell phone bill, leaving her with an additional $1,600 per year in her pocket.

Even when a hirer says, "This is our best offer," you should still take a day or two to sleep on it. More often than not, you will think of something to negotiate. Dion negotiated a start date that was one week earlier so health benefits were covered for the month, a significant savings for his family. Laura negotiated a mid-year (off-cycle) performance review, which would come with a salary increase if she met the agreed-upon business goals.

Your new employer wants you to come on board motivated to dive in. Out of all the candidates, they chose *you*. A few thousand dollars may be negligible to them, but mean the world to you. So, take 10 minutes to start off your next job with a win-win.

SWITCH ACTION

Think About Asking for Other Perks

AFTER GETTING YOUR BASE salary as high as possible, consider the total compensation. It can help fill in the financial gap between what you were hoping to be paid and what you were offered. Before the negotiation meeting, consider the following list of benefits and perks:

→ Paid time off or extra vacation

→ Annual or sign-on bonuses

→ Educational assistance/tuition expenses or loan payback

→ Insurance (life, disability, liability, medical, dental, vision, etc.)

→ Pension/401(k) contributions

→ Start date

→ Flextime/telecommuting

→ Stock options

→ Relocation expenses and taxes

→ Off-cycle salary review

→ Professional license expenses

→ Association dues/professional club memberships

→ Commuting costs (parking, etc.)

→ Overtime pay

→ Training/professional development

→ Cell phone reimbursement

→ Air travel or hotel points

→ Job responsibilities/reporting relationships

→ Title/grade level

→ Auto expenses/mileage

→ Office space/location

→ Professional assistance programs (tax, legal, finances, etc.)

→ Expense accounts

→ Resources (equipment, budget, etc.)

→ Severance package

→ Child/elder care contributions

→ Extra compensation for waiving benefit package (if spouse carries coverage)

Some companies are getting creative with their perks, offering incentives for biking to work, paying for wedding expenses, or giving free gym memberships. Companies offer them because they are relatively inexpensive, but can increase employee satisfaction and boost a positive corporate culture. So, get creative: It's okay to ask, even if it's not something the company officially offers. Rosa was getting married later that year and she negotiated an extra paid week of vacation for her honeymoon as a sign-on bonus, which was a win-win for her and the company. A perk that may be very meaningful to you, like childcare contributions or a day to work from home each week, may be something that costs the company pennies, and they are glad to have you come on board happy. If you don't ask, you'll never get it!

What's the Opposite of Failure?

Responsibility—Reality—Risk—Resilience

IF YOUR IMMEDIATE ANSWER to that question is "success," you're in good company. In our culture, the words "succeed" and "fail" are usually considered opposites. But this is a simplistic way of viewing things. Cognitively, we know there are many shades of gray between success and failure. Yet, if something doesn't go as planned, it's not uncommon to jump to the conclusion that we've failed. Didn't get the promotion? Fail. Manuscript rejected? Fail. Invention doesn't work? Fail. No offers after several interviews? Fail.

Depending on your locus of control (see Chapter Two), people have an innate tendency either to blame themselves when things go wrong (internal locus of control) or to blame someone or something else (external locus of control). Those who embrace an internal locus of control are tough on themselves when things don't turn out as anticipated. "I could have tried harder," "I should've been more prepared," and so on. But beating yourself up is not only unproductive, it's also damaging. Failure is *not* actually the opposite of success, but rather a *necessary stepping stone* to attain success. In fact, it's nearly impossible to have success without the prerequisite of failure. Failing is how we learn. It's our guidepost to course corrections and our motivation to improve. People who've attained greatness encountered several "failure stepping stones" along the way.

As a Switcher, you have a lot to learn, and regardless of how diligent you are, you will encounter setbacks. Treat those setbacks as what they really are: learning opportunities. Engaging a *growth mindset* plays a large role in your motivation to improve and keep going (a fixed mindset is what keeps you stuck).[2] So reflect on the things you've succeeded at, and you'll likely recall many "learning opportunities" that you forgot because they weren't the big deal they appeared to be.

Engage Psychology: The Simplest Negotiating Trick You'll Ever Learn

There's a lot of excellent negotiating advice available. You can find it in dozens of career books or online, so you don't need me to tell you the basics. Here's a quick synopsis:

- Defer the in-depth salary discussion until after you have an official offer in hand.
- Research your market value and how to relay it to the employer based on what you bring to the role.
- Focus on your worth in the market, not what you personally want or need, or what you were making in the last position.
- Never accept an offer on the spot, even a seemingly great offer. There's always something to negotiate.
- Negotiate directly with the hiring manager (vs. the headhunter or human resources).
- Be confident and respectful, not demanding or entitled.

- Don't drag out the negotiations over multiple meetings. Know your negotiating points and alternative options so you can be efficient.
- Know your BATNA (best alternative to a negotiated agreement) and your walk-away number.

All these steps are important. Just add this one vital strategy: *Go into the negotiation meeting assuming positive intent on the part of the hiring manager.* As Fisher and Ury point out in *Getting to Yes*, people come into negotiations recognizing the stakes are high, which fuels emotions that can ultimately lead to an impasse.[3] It's this concern that causes many candidates to skip the negotiations altogether, worry about an awkward exchange, feel afraid of annoying their new boss, or be concerned the offer will be rescinded. It also causes some candidates to enter with guns blazing in an attempt to "win." But this usually sparks a battle of egos, and even if you win, you can damage the relationship. You win the battle at the expense of the war.

You may be sending subtle signs of being on the defensive simply because you *expect* the hiring manager to push back. While it's advisable to prepare your rationale (it will give you the confidence and data support you need), you'll end up with a better outcome by going into the discussion expecting success. Hiring managers anticipate that you will negotiate. Unless your requests are completely unreasonable or presented as demands, managers likely will be happy to revise the offer if they're able. Even if they can't give you exactly what you want, ask if they can meet you in the middle. Since speaking about money is uncomfortable, treat the salary discussion as if it's any other conversation. Mary pretended she was negotiating dinner options with her husband to take the edge off—it worked!

The true art of negotiating lies mostly in *attitude*. A collaborative, positive, and reasonable negotiation is the start of a partnership. So don't be defensive or entitled; your relationship could kick off with a lack of trust and mutual respect. Entering any negotiation assuming positive intent will get you further. Approaching the negotiation as a discussion with an ally versus an adversary is your secret key to success.

Loss Aversion Revisited

While there's always room to negotiate, that doesn't mean that as a Switcher you'll end up earning exactly what you'd like. In fact, depending on how big your career change and your skill level in relation to the new job, there's a strong possibility that making a switch may mean accepting a lower salary, at least temporarily. Taking a salary hit is one of the major concerns Switchers struggle with in their decision making. While I wish I could reassure Switchers, "Of course your salary won't decrease," regrettably, whether you can stomach a pay cut is a consideration when deciding to change careers.

If you're taking a significant step back in level or changing from an industry like banking to a nonprofit, a lower salary may be inevitable. This is where your loss aversion (see Chapter Two) tends to kick in and you ask yourself, "Is this really worth it?"

Consider all the factors. Think about the long-term payoff. Will taking a hit on salary in the short run enable you to leap ahead of your old salary in the longer run? Even if that's not the case, it's likely the monetary hit won't be as painful as you envision. Research has shown that, although people aren't very good at foreseeing how they will adjust to change, people "adapt more quickly and to a larger degree than we imagine."[4]

Keep the large view of a compensation package in mind. Look at the *total* compensation. You may not be losing as much as you think if they cover tuition reimbursement and your commute requires much less gas. It's worth the extra effort to think creatively. Perhaps you have experiences that will add additional value. If your graphics design skills could save the company $5,000 annually on an external vendor, maybe they could add this amount to your salary when they hire you. Remember, if you don't ask, the answer is always no.

Consider the big picture. Salary *is* a key motivator, but other aspects of a job contribute to overall satisfaction. If your new job energizes you, reduces stress, or allows you to spend more time on hobbies that give you pleasure, perhaps the trade-off in pay is worth it.

The phenomenon of loss aversion drives people to put more weight on what they're *losing*, which often overshadows the many gains and skews the big picture. Instead of focusing on the money or status you may be foregoing, give equal weight to all you are *gaining*.

Choosing Between Two Solid Offers

Although it's a good problem to have, it can be stressful to decide between two seemingly awesome job offers, especially when there is no clear front-runner. The compensation for one job is higher, but the second job would mean an easier commute. Or, the brand name of one company is appealing, but the actual work in the other company seems more interesting—argh! You start wishing you could pick a few qualities from each offer and mush them together to create the perfect role.

Some people are tempted to allow the decision to come down to money. But take a long-term perspective. A short-term financial dip may be worth the sacrifice. You're changing careers for a reason: You want to make the right choice so you'll be happy going forward. Asking yourself some questions may help you choose.

☛ **Is your new boss going to be a good coach, advocate, sponsor, and someone you can learn from and trust?** People don't leave *companies*—a Gallup poll of over 7,200 U.S. employees

showed that one in two employees leave their *boss*.[5] Your fit
with your new boss should be weighted heavily. Future promotions, raises, and internal opportunities for growth can funnel
through this one person, not to mention your daily happiness.
As a Switcher, your need for an advocate and teacher might
be higher than a traditional candidate's. Even if all else seems
ideal, trust your instincts on this one—it could mean the difference between being groomed as a high-potential employee
or enduring pure misery.

☞ **What is your exit strategy?** It may sound strange to consider
your next role when you haven't even started *this* one. However, it's no longer the norm to stay at one company for your
entire career, so consider what opportunities this next role will
open for you. As a Switcher, think about what skill gaps you
will close in this job, who you will add to your network, and
how the experience will set you up for success at future roles.

☞ **Is fear factoring into your decision?** Emotions play a role in all
decisions, and the human brain is hardwired to steer clear of
danger (see Chapter Two). Sometimes going with what is most
comfortable makes complete sense, but often, it limits growth.
Fear of failure can be a powerful deterrent, but don't allow it
to be the deciding factor. A few months into the new job, you'll
be excelling and laughing about having worried so much. As a
Switcher, you might be tempted to go with what feels "safer,"
but test that theory with family or friends to make sure you're
not selling yourself short.

☞ **Which company's culture aligns more closely with your values?**
Your values play a huge role in satisfaction and tend to remain
relatively static throughout your lifetime (see Chapter Three).
It's possible to put values on the back burner for short periods
of time when you're pursuing a time-limited goal like earning
an MBA, but it is stressful for extended periods. Learn as much

as you can about company culture through conversations with current employees and network contacts. If autonomy and flexibility are key values for you, you'll quickly become frustrated with a "butt in chair" culture of clock watchers or with a micromanager.

👉 **Are there red flags you may be ignoring?** While a big brand name and glitzy title may be appealing on paper, it's important to assess if the job lives up to the hype. Signs to watch for include high turnover, ambiguous expectations or goals for the role, whether the position has been vacant for a long time, and whether you feel like you're being "sold" during the hiring process. As a Switcher, you might be tempted to overlook red flags to take what you can get, but it pays to listen to your intuition. Be patient and don't dismiss those warning signs, otherwise you may be right back in the job search.

The decision will still be difficult. The good news is there really isn't a right or wrong choice. One option will rise to the top, and who knows—the company you pass up may be one you're interested in pursuing in the future. So decline gracefully and stay in contact. The *great* news is you have landed a job in your new career path—way to go! So, forget what life may have been like in the role you turned down and focus on being a star in your new profession.

IN SUMMARY

Although some people enjoy haggling over prices when bargaining, when it comes to salary discussions, the conversation is personal, emotional, and abstract—and therefore inherently uncomfortable. In the case of a Switcher, it can be tempting to jump at a decent offer to be finished with the process. However, those 10 minutes of awkward conversation may put a significant amount of money in your pocket, not only over the next year but for many years to come.

CHAPTER TWELVE SWITCH POINTS

→ Hiring managers expect you to negotiate. Done respectfully, it can both increase your earnings and enhance your relationship.

→ Even if presented with a good offer, sleep on it. Chances are there is something extra—a sign-on bonus, additional vacation time, flextime—that will benefit you.

→ There are many perks that put money into your pocket at the end of the month in addition to base salary. Understand which are meaningful to you.

→ As a Switcher, you may need to take a hit on compensation; however, don't let that one factor override all the positive gains that come with the career change. Money is only one piece of the larger career-switch puzzle.

→ Choosing between two solid offers can be difficult. Consider multiple factors such as your direct boss, longer-term opportunities, and company culture when deciding.

→ Failure is a learning opportunity that is par for the career-switch course! Get up, dust off, and keep on moving forward.

Never Look for a Job Again

(Get Recruited!)

Congratulations! You've made it—you've been offered your dream job, negotiated a solid compensation, and are in employee orientation. You sent thank-you notes to all the people in your network who gave you a boost along the way (regardless of whether they were directly involved in the job you ultimately accepted), and have plans to maintain contact with your network and grow it. You've worked tirelessly to get this far so definitely celebrate, but don't let the momentum trail off. There's still work to do! You can ensure you *never need to search for a job again.* That might sound too good to be true. Never look for a job again? Really? Yes—it truly is an achievable goal. Instead of job hunting, you can create a situation where the jobs will come to you through your network. In this chapter, you will:

- Be inspired to keep pushing and challenging yourself long after your job search has successfully ended so you will be ready when future opportunities arise

- Learn how to keep building your brand even when you're happily employed
- Discover the benefits of micro-networking
- Take a moment to be grateful to the people who have helped you, and pay that gratitude forward to others
- Learn how two easy questions can keep you on track to your goal

Become the Least Qualified Person in the Room

If you want to continue to grow your career, my best advice to you is this: Continually put yourself in situations where you're *the least qualified person in the room*. As a Switcher, this is essentially what you've just done. So, you know it takes courage, it's uncomfortable, and it requires an ego release. To continue catapulting yourself toward success, put yourself into professional situations where you have some foundational knowledge, but are still a novice. And be sure the outcomes *matter*. After all, as a successful Switcher, you've already proven you can take risks and crush it! So, while anyone can attend a seminar on building the perfect sales pitch, you will go beyond this and volunteer to lead the proposal team for pitching a new client. As you know, it makes a difference when you've got skin in the game.

Also, being the least qualified person in the room means you have experts around you to learn from. It doesn't mean that you personally don't have anything to offer; rather, your list of credentials in this area may not be as impressive . . . yet. You can observe, reflect, and mirror. This is a hallmark of a growth mindset (see Chapter Two) and a strategy that athletes have used for decades. If you want to be a better swimmer, join a Masters' Swim team. Yes, you may be the slowest one in the pool at first, but progress will be made as you push to swim with the pros. Remember, your brain *wants* you to settle back into old habits and find your comfort zone again. After a major switch, don't stay there too long. It's easy to get complacent and settle for "good enough." In addition, the more competent you become in your new field, the fewer risks you will want to take. Don't listen to the seemingly logical reasons your brain stirs up and get lazy. You know what to listen for:

- "But, I've never managed people before."
- "Everyone else on the team has an advanced degree except me."
- "I don't know enough about the industry [or client or project]."
- "I'll hold everyone else back."
- "I'm not ready.

If you want to fast-track your career, you need to S-T-R-E-T-C-H outside of your comfort zone regularly. All your reasons may be true (maybe this *is* your first time leading a team), but *none* of them indicates that you won't be successful. Don't turn down an opportunity that you want, but that scares you. Once you adjust to the new challenge and figure out how to tackle it, you'll become such a pro that you'll be kicking yourself for not diving in sooner.

SWITCH ACTION

Draw on Your Past Experiences with Risk Taking

THE FIRST TIME I hosted *Career Talk* on Sirius XM radio in 2015, I was visibly shaking and could barely form coherent sentences. I had zero background in broadcasting and knew that my performance was being evaluated to determine if the producers wanted to add *Career Talk* as a regularly featured program (not to mention the show was live and being broadcast across North

America!). Fast-forward three years, and hosting the show is truly the highlight of my week.

Consider a time when you were afraid to try something because there was the possibility you might fail, but once you jumped in, you turned out to be successful. Pick something that has relatively high stakes, such as moving to a new city on your own, giving a public speech, accepting a challenging promotion, or performing onstage. Now pull out your journal and answer these questions, putting thought into your responses and being as specific as possible:

→ What were you most fearful about?
→ Which of those fears actually came to pass?
→ How did you handle it?
→ What did you learn about your ability to handle new (and potentially scary) situations?
→ How can you use this experience in the future to advance your career?

Stop wondering how other people are getting the great opportunities and fast-track *your* career by continuing to seek out situations where:

→ Your qualifications are budding, but not at mastery level yet.
→ You have some accountability or stake in the game so the outcomes matter.
→ You're surrounded by people more qualified than you in this field or skill who you can learn from.

If your goals are important to you, self-doubt will creep in each time you contemplate jumping into the next big pond. This is an indicator that you're moving in exactly the right direction!

Brand Deposits

Whether you're happily employed or in a job transition, part of any successful career management strategy is building your brand so others automatically associate you with your area of expertise. Your brand is your reputation. It is how others experience you and what behaviors they come to expect of you professionally. It's the problems you solve and how you go about solving them. You've worked very hard to rebrand for this career switch, and continuing to brand is important.

Brand deposits are small, consistent actions that reinforce and strengthen your brand positively with your audience. As discussed in Chapter Five, Steve Jobs coined this term for how companies build strong reputations, likening brand building to a bank account. Positive customer experiences lead to brand *deposits*, while negative experiences lead to brand *withdrawals*. Having an excess of deposits allows a company to have a few setbacks without too much damage to the overall reputation.[1]

This concept works with individuals as well. No one is perfect, but actions speak louder than words and people are paying attention. From the content you post on social media, to how you introduce yourself to others at a conference, to your body language in the staff meeting, becoming conscious about making brand deposits will pave the way for a successful future. Over time, your reputation will precede you. Others will speak favorably about your skills, contributions, or expertise, and more opportunities will flow your way.

These brand reinforcers don't need to be major efforts; actions like showing up on time and prepared, following through on commitments to maintain credibility, being consistent with contributions in your area of expertise, and welcoming others with warmth and generosity can go a long way. Once your brand is established, small positive actions can have massive impact over time. Why is this important? Here are just a few benefits to maintaining a strong brand:

☛ Chances are, you'll eventually find yourself in another job search. If you're well-known for a skill or area of expertise, you'll already have credibility with your network and will be one step ahead of the curve.

☛ When people think of you as the "go-to" person in your industry or specialty, you'll gain a following, including respect from your competition. Staying "top of mind" is important.

☛ If you're in a field where you have clients or buyers, or are working as an independent consultant, brand recognition is the key to growth and future leads.

☛ In an organization, building a positive reputation and expertise leads to better opportunities. When people you don't know well start seeking you out for your expertise, you'll know you have an effective brand.

When you're not actively in a job search, building your brand doesn't have to take hours. This is where small brand deposits come into play to subtly keep you in front of your network.

Become Your Brand

While humans are multidimensional, on a professional level it makes sense to become known for your expertise and the problems you solve. For example, as a career coach, when someone wants to switch careers, I want to be the first person they think to call. As your new brand solidifies, what is it you want to be known for in professional circles? The answer should be consistently tethered to you so others easily make this connection. These strategies offer a big bang for your buck in terms of becoming known for your specialty:

1. Add a custom signature to your email account. Include a few key words about your area of expertise, a hyperlink to your professional page or website, and possibly a favorite quote. This way, each time someone gets a correspondence from you, they'll link you to your brand.

2. Always carry business cards and, to the extent your company allows, include a few key words about your expertise. If you don't have cards through a company or are still in school, you can create some for a very low cost. Sharing contact information is essential, so keep a few spare business cards in your smartphone case as backup.

3. When you meet people, they often ask, "What do you do?" Instead of answering with, "I work at Amazon," or "I'm in marketing," be specific about your field and the value you bring. For example, "I'm a communications strategist in the marketing department at Amazon and my role focuses on how to promote the company's image in the media, specifically around charitable giving."

4. When you run into contacts you haven't seen in a while and they ask how you are, give a detailed answer such as "They have been lots of changes since we last spoke. I've transitioned into direct sales at a global tech firm where I'm building their Southwest region," rather than a canned "Things are great . . .". Don't miss the many daily opportunities to strengthen your brand.

While there are many other formal strategies for strengthening your brand, the four strategies above take little effort, and go a long way in helping people to associate your name with your expertise.

One Thing to Start, One Thing to Stop

Responsibility—Reality—Risk—Resilience

WHEN LIFE IS MOVING at warp speed, it's easy to fall into a pattern of doing things that *feel* productive, but don't actually move you toward your goals. My favorite term for this is "active laziness"—the habit of filling life with tasks that make us *feel* needed and productive, but simply enable us to avoid those challenging tasks that would move us toward our true goals.

I personally hate to slow down, but I recognize the importance of taking time to reflect on what I'm doing to ensure I'm moving in directions that most align with my goals, rather than being a zombie to learned habits (the brain is an expert at keeping us tied to habits, even long after they no longer serve us). To keep on track toward your goals, ask these two basic questions on a quarterly basis:

- What is one thing I can *stop* doing today that will have a significant impact on my life?
- What is one thing I can *start* doing today that will have a significant impact on my life?

Addicted to reruns? You could remove the batteries from the remote control (to *stop* being distracted from the job search) and *start* taking one daily action on social media each morning to strengthen your brand. Maybe you *stop* eating lunch at your desk and *start* meeting new people in the building lunchroom twice each week instead. Some of these decisions will be life-changing, and others will make life more productive for a while. Not all changes will "stick"; in some cases, the behavior change is "time-bound," and it isn't critical (or helpful) to continue indefinitely.

Each time we slow down enough to ask ourselves these two questions, we have the chance to consciously redirect our choices to ensure they align with our long-term goals, and not just our short-term desires. Every day is a chance for a new beginning. What will yours be?

Micro-Networking

It seems like everything's going "micro" these days—loans, breweries, even homes—so why not networking? Micro-networking is like brand deposits: a simple, efficient way to cultivate your existing network through "mini-yet-meaningful" interactions. Micro-networking strengthens current relationships and forms foundations for new ones when you're not in an active job search.

Research suggests it can take potential customers up to two years to trust a company brand, and trust is key to standing out over the competition.[2] Repeated, consistent exchanges are also important in building personal relationships (because outta sight, outta mind!). Baber and Waymon estimate that it takes six to eight interactions demonstrating reliable behaviors with contacts to establish trust.[3]

With a busy schedule (and a new job!), it can be challenging to find time for lunch meetings or business social events each month. However, this isn't a reason to let your contacts grow cold. Micro-networking is a way to keep your established relationships fresh and more quickly strengthen newer connections, while building your brand and helping others, all in just minutes a day. Here are some ways you can add it to your routine:

- Take a few minutes during the week to endorse contacts on social media or "like" or retweet their content. They'll receive a notification letting them know you did it.

- Repost useful articles summarizing the content to save your contacts' time. It will inform your audience, while reinforcing your brand.

- Attend events where you'll see several people in your network at once like a wedding, reunion, holiday event, or retirement party. Then be sure to make the rounds. Just a few minutes of face time with current contacts can significantly strengthen the relationships.

☞ Become a superconnector. Introduce your contacts to others in your network who have aligned interests or goals. This will help both of your contacts expand their network circles, with *you* as a common thread.

☞ Keep track of birthdays or other special events and "ping" your contacts on those days. Many social media sites and apps automatically track this information, so there's no need to rely on memory. Just point and click!

☞ Bring cookies to the monthly meeting once in a while to spark interactions or place a candy jar on your desk to encourage others to stop by.

☞ When you run into someone you know, *mean it* when you ask, "How are things?" Listen for ways to strengthen the connection or help them out. In turn, be prepared to respond with more detail than "Same old, same old" when they ask you "what's new?" Share the new project you've been selected to lead at work or your recent promotion.

Micro-networking tends to be most useful for maintaining current relationships, but building new contacts doesn't take much effort if you're curious enough to sit next to someone you don't know at the next company-wide town hall meeting. Before you know it, your brain will make micro-networking a habit.

Pay It Forward

In a recent study on employment, only 14 percent of respondents indicated they had "received help of any kind from others" in attaining their new job.[4] Since it has been well known for decades that people land most jobs (60 to 80 percent) through networking, this study implies most people *forget* that other people helped them find employment. In a world where information is constantly streaming and interactions are constantly happening, it's getting easier to forget who did what. Like the person who introduced you to a connection, who turned into a lucrative client. Or the person who posted the article that motivated you to take a chance on a new venture. Or the great advice you got from a colleague at lunch that inspired you to sign up for that class. Or the feedback you received from a previous boss that ultimately led to a future promotion.

Everything we have and everything we do is connected to other people, and as a successful Switcher, you've likely come to understand that firsthand. When we take a moment to examine who we are and what we have achieved, people helped us all along the way. Although the encouragement, advice, and input may be subtle, others are constantly there, guiding us to our next steps.

So take a moment to think about the people in your life that you appreciate. Why not send them a quick email to let them know how they influenced your life for the better? Your "thank you" may be the encouragement they need to achieve something great today.

It's also important to look ahead, to pay that gratitude forward to others, especially since you know firsthand how challenging the career-switch journey can be. Networking is about building relationships, and one of the best ways to do that is to help your contacts achieve *their* goals. Adam Grant's research in *Give and Take* shows that "givers" are among those at the top of the success ladder,[5] so paying it forward is how we can all rise up. Here are 10 easy ways to pay your gratitude forward to your contacts:

1. Introduce them to someone in your network who may be a mutually beneficial contact.

2. Invite them to a networking, social, or professional event they might find interesting.

3. Write a testimonial your contact can post or use for marketing brochures, or write a recommendation for your contact on LinkedIn.

4. Promote your contacts' successes (awards, media appearances, speaking engagements) and their content, upcoming gigs, or job openings within your network.

5. Share a powerful article or resource on social media that provides insightful professional information others may find useful.

6. Refer a potential client to your contact or pass along her business card to someone who might be interested in her services or products.

7. Listen for potential professional (job openings, vendors) and personal (a new dentist, a reputable roofer, a reliable babysitter) needs and make recommendations when able.

8. Share news, non-proprietary competitor information, and ideas you come across that are relevant to your contact's field or business.

9. Help a fellow Switcher. Now that you know the challenges and have the best strategies for defeating the obstacles, share this book and your knowledge with others starting this journey.

10. Simply ask others how you can help. Sometimes this is the easiest way to find out what would be most useful to your contacts.

In the words of Zig Ziglar, "You will get all you want in life, if you help enough other people get what they want."[6]

IN SUMMARY

As a successful Switcher, you've navigated a tough road and have overcome many real challenges and imaginary (but no less powerful) fears to attain your goal. And if you're not quite there yet, you're learning how to make your goal a reality through the strategies and advice in this book. So, congratulations are in order!

I have seen people walk away from their career dreams. Some can't overcome fear of loss, be it loss of status, money, or professional identity. Others carved a solid path, but got defeated and gave up too soon. Some spent so much energy searching for "fairness," they had nothing left for learning to maneuver within reality. Victorious Switchers, like all flourishing professionals, are rarely an overnight success. These obstacles are significant, but are they more significant than realizing your career goals? Only you can decide. And if you choose to forge ahead, I'm confident that with persistence, planning, and patience, you'll become a successful Switcher. Happy hunting!

CHAPTER THIRTEEN SWITCH POINTS

→ You've overcome and learned a lot during your Switch journey—keep it up. Continue to stretch yourself professionally by finding opportunities to be the least qualified person in the room.

→ Branding and networking are ongoing activities for successful professionals. Career management isn't an occasional event. Find ways to micro-network and make brand deposits to strengthen your reputation in the market.

→ Take time to slow down and evaluate how your actions are influencing your career goals. There may be things you can start or stop doing that will have a major impact on your success.

→ Don't forget how you got where you are. Keep your eyes open for chances to help others attain career success. None of us are successful without the support of others.

Appendix

How to Choose a Career Coach

If you've implemented the advice I've offered in this book and your job search still isn't picking up traction in the way you'd like, it might be time to consider working with a professional career coach. A few simple strategy tweaks may be all you need to bust through what's blocking you.

First, it's important to understand the role of a career coach. They are not headhunters, therapists, or placement professionals, but rather skilled advisors who help you to hone your brand, materials (i.e., resume, cover letters), and job search strategy, as well as assist you in evaluating your networking techniques, practicing interviews, and building confidence through feedback and insight. Often, they are former recruiters or placement professionals from the "other side of the desk" who now share their insider tips with job seekers.

Choosing the right coach might feel daunting. How do you know who's qualified? Who will help put you on the path toward your goals? Are they legit or just out to make a quick buck? Just like when you're picking a preschool for your daughter or a centrally located hotel for your trip to London, word of mouth and personal recommendations are the best way to find a compatible coach. If you have no leads, a good place to begin might be the career center from your university. They may offer services to alumni or have external coaches they recommend.

Failing that, the internet is likely your next best bet. Unfortunately, there is a lot of information to sift through online, so here are a few key criteria to help guide your decision.

☛ **Expertise and Background.** While it isn't necessary for a coach to have direct work experience in the industry/function you are pursuing, it can be helpful if the coach has successfully worked with clients in related areas. As a Switcher, you will want a coach who has helped others transition into new careers and who understands the need to rebrand. Also, a prior background in recruiting or executive search enables a coach to understand the employer's perspective, which can be incredibly valuable as you navigate the hiring process.

☛ **Style/Approach.** As with any partnership, fit is a key ingredient for success. Consider what would be most helpful to you: flexibility, structure, an accountability partner? Some coaches have set programs and packages, while others tailor services to your individual preferences. Interview a few coaches so you can choose one who's a good match for your needs and work style. Don't feel compelled to purchase an extensive three-month package if you just want a resume review. That said, it often takes three to four sessions to assess a job seeker's potential challenges and create a strategy, so don't skimp either. This may be one of the most important investments you make in yourself.

☛ **Knowledge/Education.** An advanced degree or specialized certification doesn't automatically make someone an expert. In the same way, a lack of certain credentials doesn't necessarily mean someone isn't a skilled coach. Go beyond the letters after the name. Ask for recommendations, and check out the coach's website and online presence. Does he contribute to the field (via blogs, articles, discussions, etc.)? Does she stay current? Is the coach willing to provide referrals or testimonials of individuals in your (or a similar) situation?

☞ Free consultation and an attitude of candor. For many job seekers, career coaching is a foreign concept. Coaches should be willing to answer questions and offer a brief consultation at no charge to ensure they can help you to achieve your specific goals. Not every coach will be a good match, and you both deserve the opportunity to figure that out before entering a contract. If you feel rushed to decide or pressured into purchasing something you don't want or can't afford, walk away.

☞ Tech savvy and on the leading edge of the field. Social media and a strong online brand are no longer optional in a career search. Select a coach who stays updated on current trends and has a decent website where you can learn more about the service offerings. Ask what the coach does to keep up with the latest job search strategies and what part of the career coaching process he focuses on (e.g., exploration, job search tools, interview prep). Is career coaching only a small part of the business or the primary focus? This may not be a deal breaker, but it's something to consider. Job search trends continuously change, so it's important for coaches to keep up.

☞ Making Guarantees? A lot of external factors play into whether you're offered a new position (e.g., industry, level, location, skill set, market, economy, etc.), so be wary of coaches who promise you a job. Even with a great coach, you'll still be shouldering the heavy lifting; if it sounds too good to be true, it probably is. Each client is unique, so one client's experience could be different from the next. Instead of false promises, coaches should seek to gain clarity about your goals and any tangible results you desire from the partnership (i.e., you want your coach to help rebrand your resume, hone in on a career choice, etc.). Explicitly contracting expectations and outcomes up front will ensure that incorrect assumptions don't get in the way of a successful partnership.

☛ Practicalities. Don't overlook the practical aspects of the coaching process, such as the coach's office location (many work virtually via phone or Skype, which can be equally effective and very convenient, especially if you're working and can't make in-person meetings), schedule availability (weekdays only?), the cost (set price? hourly?), and the methods of payment accepted. For example, coaches who only offer extensive packages may not be a fit if you just want to do a mock interview. While it's not uncommon for coaches to require some payment up front, don't be shy about asking for a payment plan if that better suits your needs.

Your career coach will be partnering with you on a very important aspect of your life. In addition to the above criteria, you should get a sense that the individual is passionate about coaching and genuinely cares about your success. Do your homework, but trust your gut. It won't lead you astray.

NOTES

PREFACE

1. "Number of Jobs Held in a Lifetime," U.S. Department of Labor, Bureau of Labor Statistics, last modified February 9, 2017, https://www.bls.gov/nls/nlsfaqs.htm#anch41.

CHAPTER 1

1. Barry Schwartz, *The Paradox of Choice: Why More is Less* (Brilliance Audio; Unabridged edition, 2014).
2. Tony Robbins, *Awaken the Giant Within: How to Take Immediate Control of Your Mental, Emotional, Physical and Financial Destiny!* (New York: Simon & Schuster, 2007), p. 49.

CHAPTER 2

1. Neil Pasricha, *The Happiness Equation: Want Nothing + Do Anything = Have Everything* (New York, NY: G.P. Putnam's Sons, 2016).
2. Rick Hanson and Richard Mendius, *Buddha's Brain: The Practical Neuroscience of Happiness, Love and Wisdom* (Oakland, CA: New Harbinger, 2009).
3. Frederick B. Wilcox, *A Little Book of Aphorisms* (New York: Scribner, 1947).
4. Joan Duncan Oliver, *Commit to Sit: Tools for Cultivating a Meditation Practice from the Pages of Tricycle* (Carlsbad, CA: Hay House, 2009).
5. Herminia Ibarra, *Working Identity: Unconventional Strategies for Reinventing Your Career* (Cambridge, MA: Harvard Business Review Press, 2003).
6. William Bridges, *Managing Transitions: Making the Most of Change* (Boston: Addison Wesley, 1991).
7. Daniel Kahneman and Amos Tversky, *"Choices, Values, and Frames," American Psychologist 39, 4 (1984): 341–350.*
8. Dan Ariely, *The Upside of Irrationality: The Unexpected Benefits of Defying Logic at Work and at Home* (New York: Harper, 2010), p. 285.

9.   Christina Staudt and J. Harold Ellens, *Our Changing Journey to the End: Reshaping Death, Dying, and Grief in America* (Westport, CT: Praeger, 2013), p. 56.

10. Walter Mischel et al., "Cognitive and Attentional Mechanisms in Delay of Gratification," *Journal of Personality and Social Psychology,* 21 (1972): 204–218.

11. Fred Yager, "The Cost of Bad Hiring Decisions Runs High," Dice, http://insights.dice.com/report/the-cost-of-bad-hiring-decisions/.

12. Tom Tassinari and Michele Tassinari, *Top 5 Hiring Mistakes & How to Fix Them* (Phoenix, AZ: Synergy Solutions, 2009).

13. F. Leigh Branham, "Six Truths About Employee Turnover," American Management Association, June 7, 2004, http://www.nichebenefits.com/library/sixtruths.pdf.

14. Karie Willyerd, "What High Performers Want at Work," *Harvard Business Review,* November 18, 2014, https://hbr.org/2014/11/what-high-performers-want-at-work.

15. Anthony Damasio, *Descartes' Error: Emotion, Reason, and the Human Brain* (New York: Penguin, 2005).

16. "Trust Your Gut: Intuitive Decision-Making Based on Expertise May Deliver Better Results Than Analytical Approach," *ScienceDaily,* December 20, 2012, www.sciencedaily.com/releases/2012/12/121220144155.htm.

17. *The Arts Go To School: Classroom-based activities that focus on music, painting, drama, movement, media, and more,* Edited by David Booth and Masayuki Hachiya, (Sidebar quotation) (Pembroke Publishers, Markham, Ontario, 2004), p. 14.

18. Seth Godin: Confusing Signals Blog, October 8, 2017, http://sethgodin.typepad.com/seths_blog/.

19. Carol S. Dweck, *Mindset: The New Psychology of Success (*New York: Ballantine Books, Rep Upd edition, 2007).

20. Angela Duckworth, *Grit: The Power of Passion and Perseverance* (New York: Scribner, 2016).

21. Jia Jiang, *Rejection Proof: How I Beat Fear and Became Invincible Through 100 Days of Rejection* (New York: Harmony Books, 2015), p. 212.

CHAPTER 3

1.   Peter Dinklage. Commencement Speech, Bennington College, Class of 2012.

2.   *The Bhagavad Gita* (Penguin Classics; Revised edition, 2003).

3. Jack Canfield and Mark Victor Hansen. *Chicken Soup for the Soul* (Health Communications, Inc.; Revised edition, 1993).

4. Jihae Shin and Katherine L. Milkman, "How Backup Plans Can Harm Goal Pursuit: The Unexpected Downside of Being Prepared for Failure," *Organizational Behavior and Human Decision Processes* 135 (2016): 1–9.

5. Julie Cohen, *Your Work, Your Life . . . Your Way: 7 Keys to Work–Life Balance* (Philadelphia: Julie Cohen Coaching, 2009).

6. Cliff Sims, "Mike Rowe's Must-Read Response to an Alabamian Who Asked Why He Shouldn't Follow His Passion," *Yellow Hammer,* October 1, 2014, http://yellowhammernews.com/faithandculture/ alabamian-gets-schooled-mike-rowe-dirty-jobs/.

CHAPTER 4

1. SHRM 2016 Annual Conference in Washington DC, June 19–22, 2016.

CHAPTER 5

1. Joe Dispenza, *Evolve Your Brain: The Science of Changing Your Mind* (Florida: HCI, 2008).

2. Douglas Stone et al., *Difficult Conversations: How to Discuss What Matters Most* (New York: Penguin, 2000).

3. Ken Segall, *Insanely Simple: The Obsession That Drives Apple's Success* (New York: Portfolio, 2012).

CHAPTER 6

1. Sheiresa Ngo, "Job Advice: Do You Need to Be Liked at Work to Succeed?" *Money & Career Cheat Sheet*, October 16, 2016, http://www .cheatsheet.com/money-career/job-advice-importance-likeable-work .html/?a=viewall.

2. A LEAGUE OF THEIR OWN © 1992 Columbia Pictures Industries, Inc. All Rights Reserved. Courtesy of Columbia Pictures.

3. Chad A. Higgins and Timothy A. Judge, "The Effect of Applicant Influ-ence Tactics on Recruiter Perceptions of Fit and Hiring Recommenda-tions: A Field Study," *Journal of Applied Psychology*, 2004, Vol. 89, No. 4, 622–632; *Harvard Business Review*, "How Venture Capitalists Really Assess a Pitch," May–June 2017.

4. Amy Cuddy, *Presence: Bringing Your Boldest Self to Your Biggest Challenges* (New York: Little Brown & Company, 2016).

5. Diana I. Tamir and Jason P. Mitchell, "Disclosing Information about the Self Is Intrinsically Rewarding," PNAS 2012 109 (21) 8038–8043.

CHAPTER 7

1. "How to Rethink the Candidate Experience and Make Better Hires," *Career Builder*, June 8, 2016, http://resources.careerbuilder.com/guides/candidate-experience-guide

2. Meridith Levinson. "5 insider secrets for beating applicant tracking systems (ATS)," CIO, March 1, 2012, https://www.cio.com/article/2398753/careers-staffing/careers-staffing-5-insider-secrets-for-beating-applicant-tracking-systems.html.

3. Sajid Farooq, "Google Flooded With 70,000 Resumes," NBC Bay Area, February 10, 2011, http://www.nbcbayarea.com/blogs/press-here/Google-Flooded-With-70000-Resumes-115292179.html.

4. "How to Reduce Your Cost-to-Hire Conversion with a Successful Employee Referral Program," Jobvite, http://web.jobvite.com/rs/jobvite/images/Jobvite_SuccessfulEmployeeReferralProgram.pdf.

5. Gerry Crispin and Mark Mehler, "CareerXroads Source of Hire Report 2014: A CareerXroads 'Lab' Report: Filling the Gaps," September 2014, http://www.careerxroads.com/news/2014_SourceOfHire.pdf.

6. John Sumser, "The Odds of Getting a Job With a Recruiter," *HR Examiner,* May 4, 2011, http://www.hrexaminer.com/the-odds-of-getting-a-job-with-a-recruiter/.

7. Nick Corcodilos, "Headhunters Find People, not Jobs," Ask the Headhunter, http://www.asktheheadhunter.com/headhunters-find-people-not-jobs.

8. "Keeping an Eye on Recruiter Behavior: New Study Clarifies Recruiter Decision Making," The Ladders, https://cdn.theladders.net/static/images/basicSite/pdfs/TheLadders-EyeTracking-StudyC2.pdf; Will Evans, "You Have 6 Seconds to Make an Impression: How Recruiters See Your Resume," The Ladders, https://www.theladders.com/career-advice/you-only-get-6-seconds-of-fame-make-it-count/.

9. Jakob Nielsen, "F-Shaped Pattern for Reading Web Content," Nielsen Norman Group, April 17, 2006, https://www.nngroup.com/articles/f-shaped-pattern-reading-web-content/; "How People Read on the Web: The Eyetracking Evidence," Nielsen Norman Group, https://www.nngroup.com/reports/how-people-read-web-eyetracking-evidence/.

10. Clare Whitmell, "What Makes A Recruiter Hate Your CV?" *The Guardian*, Tuesday 8 April 2014, https://www.theguardian.com/careers/careers-blog/recruiter-hate-cv-new-job-application.

CHAPTER 8

1. Mark S. Granovetter, "The Strength of Weak Ties," *American Journal of Sociology* 78 (1973): 1360–1380.

2. SBA Office of Advocacy (September 2012), https://www.sba.gov/sites/default/files/FAQ_Sept_2012.pdf.

3. Steve Dalton, *The Two-Hour Job Search: Using Technology to Get the Right Job Faster* (New York: Ten Speed Press, 2012).

4. Adam Grant, *Give and Take: A Revolutionary Approach to Success.* (New York: Penguin Group, 2013).

5. Carmen Nobel, "Professional Networking Makes People Feel Dirty," Harvard Business School, February 9, 2015, http://hbswk.hbs.edu/item/professional-networking-makes-people-feel-dirty.

6. "How to Rethink the Candidate Experience and Make Better Hires," Career Builder, June 8, 2016, http://resources.careerbuilder.com/guides/candidate-experience-guide.

7. Andrew O'Connell, "Most People Forget That Others Helped Them Get Employment," *Harvard Business Review,* May 16, 2013, https://hbr.org/daily-stat/2013/05/most-people-forget-that-others.html.

8. Jeffrey C. Wood, *The Cognitive Behavioral Therapy Workbook for Personality Disorders: A Step-by-Step Program* (Oakland, CA: New Harbinger, 2010).

9. Susan Cain, *Quiet: The Power of Introverts in a World That Can't Stop Talking* (New York: Crown, 2011).

10. Marti Olsen Laney, *The Introvert Advantage: How to Thrive in an Extroverted World* (New York: Workman, 2002), p. 43.

11. Ibid., 10.

12. Amy Cuddy, *Presence: Bringing Your Boldest Self to Your Biggest Challenges* (Boston: Little, Brown and Company, 2015).

13. Phillip G. Zimbardo, *Shyness: What It Is, What to Do About It* (Reading, MA: Addison-Wesley, 1977).

14. Dawn Marie Graham, "The Impact of Networking Skills Training on Job Search Behaviors and Attitudes of Graduate Students Relative to Personality" (doctoral dissertation, University of Denver, 2007).

CHAPTER 9

1. Mark S. Granovetter, "The Strength of Weak Ties," *American Journal of Sociology* 78 (1973): 1360–1380.

2. Steve Dalton, *The Two-Hour Job Search: Using Technology to Get the Right Job Faster* (New York: Ten Speed Press, 2012).

3. Dale Carnegie, *How to Win Friends and Influence People* (New York: Simon and Schuster, 1936).

4. Jarawan Sakulku and James Alexander, "The Imposter Phenomenon," *International Journal of Behavior Science* 6 (2011): 73–92.

CHAPTER 10

1. Chad A. Higgins and Timothy A. Judge, "The Effect of Applicant Influence Tactics on Recruiter Perceptions of Fit and Hiring Recommendations: A Field Study," *Journal of Applied Psychology* 89 (2004): 622–632.
2. Christopher Ingraham, "America's Top Fears: Public Speaking, Heights and Bugs," Wonkblog, *Washington Post,* October 30, 2014, https://www.washingtonpost.com/news/wonk/wp/2014/10/30/clowns-are-twice-as-scary-to-democrats-as-they-are-to-republicans/?utm_term=.445a6cd75dc9.
3. Eleanor Roosevelt, *You Learn by Living: Eleven Keys for a More Fulfilling Life,* (Harper Perennial, New York; Reprint edition, 2016), p. 25.
4. Todd Bermont, *10 Insider Secrets to Job Hunting Success! Everything You Need to Get the Job You Want in 24 Hours—or Less!* (Houston: 10 Step, 2001).
5. Geoff Smart and Randy Street, *Who: The A Method for Hiring* (New York: Ballantine Books, 2008), p. 11.

CHAPTER 11

1. Debbie Ford, *The Secret of the Shadow: The Power of Owning Your Whole Story* (New York: HarperCollins, 2002), p. 83.
2. Careerealism online Poll, January 2013, https://www.workitdaily.com/application-interview-ratio/.
3. Jacquelyn Smith, "Treating Job Applicants Badly May Cost Employers Later On," *Forbes,* June 20, 2012, http://www.forbes.com/sites/jacquelynsmith/2012/06/20/new-survey-finds-that-bad-applicant-experiences-hurt-you-as-an-employer/#2060816f5f28.
4. Jia Jiang, *Rejection Proof: How I Beat Fear and Became Invincible Through 100 Days of Rejection* (New York: Harmony Books, 2015): p. 212.
5. Steve Dalton, *The Two-Hour Job Search: Using Technology to Get the Right Job Faster* (New York: Ten Speed Press, 2012).

CHAPTER 12

1. Michelle Marks and Crystal Harold, "Who Asks and Who Receives in Salary Negotiation," *Journal of Organizational Behavior* 32 (2011): 371–394.
2. Carol S. Dweck, *Mindset: The New Psychology of Success* (New York: Ballantine Books, 2008).
3. Roger Fisher and William Ury, *Getting to Yes: Negotiating Agreement without Giving In* (New York: Penguin 1991), p.100.

4. Dan Ariely, *The Upside of Irrationality: The Unexpected Benefits of Defying Logic at Work and at Home* (New York: Harper, 2010), p.160.
5. Jim Harter and Amy Adkins, Gallup Business Journal, April 8, 2015. http://news.gallup.com/businessjournal/182321/employees-lot-managers .aspx.

CHAPTER 13

1. Ken Segall, *Insanely Simple: The Obsession That Drives Apple's Success*, Kindle edition (New York: Portfolio, 2012).
2. Catherine Clifford, "How Long Before Your Customers Trust You? Two Years," *Entrepreneur*, September 17, 2014, https://www.entrepreneur .com/article/237579.
3. Anne Baber and Lynne Waymon, *Make Your Contacts Count: Networking Know-How for Business and Career Success* (New York: AMACOM, 2002), p. 49.
4. Andrew O'Connell, "Most People Forget That Others Helped Them Get Employment," *Harvard Business Review,* May 16, 2013, https://hbr.org/ daily-stat/2013/05/most-people-forget-that-others.html.
5. Adam Grant, *Give and Take: A Revolutionary Approach to Success.* (New York: Penguin Group, 2013).
6. Zig Ziglar, *Secrets of Closing the Sale: For Anyone Who Must Get Others to Say Yes!* (New York: Berkley, 1985).

INDEX